THE
Progress of SIN:
OR, THE
TRAVELS
OF
Ungodliness.

WHEREIN
The Pedigree, Rise, (or Original) Antiquity, Subtilty, Evil Nature, and Prevailing Power of SIN is fully Discovered. In an Apt and Pleasant ALLEGORY.

TOGETHER WITH
The Great Victories he hath obtained, and the Abominable Evil he hath done to Mankind, by the Help of the Devil in all his Travels, from the Beginning of the World, to this very Day.

ALSO
The Manner of his Apprehension, Arraignment, Trial, Condemnation, and Execution.

With PICTURES.

Sixth Edition, Corrected, with some Additions by the Author.

By BENJAMIN KEACH, Author of the Travels of True Godliness, War with the Devil, And ZION in Distress.

LONDON: Printed for W. JOHNSTON, at the Golden-Ball, in Ludgate-Street. 1763.

BOOKS Printed for W. Johnston, the Golden-Ball, in Ludgate-Street.

THE Great Assize: Or, Day of Jubilee: which We must make a General Account of all our Actions before the Awful Throne of GOD. Delivered in Four Sermons on the Chapter of the Revelation: Plainly the State of the Godly, and the Woeful Wicked. By Samuel Smith, late Minister at Prittlewell in Essex, Author of David's

2. David's Repentance: Or, A Plain Exposition on the LIII. Psalm: first Preached Published for the Benefit of GOD's Church every Christian may set before his Eyes the Unfeigned Repentance. Likewise Exhorting all to labour for Repentance before Sickness upon them; for that after Death there is to be had or expected. By Samuel Smith of the Word at Prittlewell in Essex, Author Great Assize.

3. Come and Welcome to Jesus Christ. and Profitable Discourse on John VI. Ver. the Cause, Truth, and Manner of the Coming ner to Jesus Christ: With his Happy Reception and Entertainment. By John Bunyan, Author Pilgrim's Progress.

4. Solomon's Temple Spiritualized: Or, fetched out of the Temple at Jerusalem, to let us easily into the Glory of New-Testament-Truths John Bunyan.

5. The Barren Fig-Tree: Or, The Downfall of the Fruitless Professor. Shewing the Day of Grace may be past with Him long his Life is Ended. The Signs also by which miserable Mortals may be known. By John

THE PREFACE.

Christian READER,

...ve lately Written a Small Treatise,
...ed, The Travels of TRUE
...LINESS, which (as I hear)
...with kind Acceptance generally amongst
...of Protestants, whether Conformists,
...conformists, I am not without Hopes
...will meet with the like; the sole or
...design of it, being to beat down Sin,
...ing forth the abominable Nature and
...hereof; together with the Wiles and
...tratagems of the Devil, to deceive the
...Men. I have in it made use of the
...Methods I did before, viz. Presenting
...have said Allegorically; which Way
...d) the Holy Ghost by the Prophets,
...the Lord JESUS Himself much de-
...d in, and made use of: For all He spoke
...the Multitude, was by Parables, &c.
...indeed, had I not Warrant from GOD's
...rd thus to Write, I should not presume so
...: I have endeavoured to avoid all Oc-
...m of Offence to all Sorts of People, not

A 3   *respecting*

The PREFACE.

reflecting on any Man's Person, whether High or Low, &c. And therefore I hope none will be offended with me, although all Kind of Sin are justly exposed, and Sinners reprehended though (may be) some will Quarrel with my very Title, and object, How can Sin be said to Travel to and fro? &c. To which I answer, Notwithstanding Sin be a Domestic Enemy, yet as Satan is said to go to and fro in the Earth, &c. to Tempt, Intice, and Draw Men into Sin, being a cunning Observer of every Man's Temper, Calling, and Inclinations; so Sin, upon this Account, I presume may be represented as a Traveller also.

I shall say no more, but leave it to the Blessing of GOD, whose Glory, I hope, I seek and desire to promote in all Things.

Reader, Tho' 'tis true, there are Books (thou may'st say) enough already; yet bear with me this once: Which is all I crave, for an Interest in thy Prayers at the Throne of Grace;

Who am thy Soul's Friend

April 28th,
1684.
                          B. KEA

THE
Progress of SIN:
OR, THE
TRAVELS
OF
𝔘𝔫𝔤𝔬𝔡𝔩𝔦𝔫𝔢𝔰𝔰.

CHAP. I.
Shewing the Pedigree, Rise, Antiquity, *and* Original *of* SIN.

ALTHOUGH *Sin*, in a proper Sense, is a *Non-Entity*; rather the Depravation of a *Being*, than a *Being* at all; yet it would be well for Thousands, yea, Millions of Thousands, if there were no such *Being* for *Sin* in their Hearts, nor in the World, as there is. What *Sin* is, the Holy Apostle

Apostle shews, viz. *The Transgression of the Law*, &c. Doing what God forbids, or not doing wh[at] God requires; or doing of it in other Mann[er] than He in his Holy Word directs, is alike Ev[il]. And in these Three Things doth *Sin* consist: The[se] are the principal Parts of that Ugly Body, or Hate[-] ful Monster, who is the Subject of this ensui[ng] History: And we hope none will be offended w[ith] [i]t, because in this Allegorical Discourse *Sin* is presented as a Person; sith the Apostle himse[lf] gives it the Name of Body, and also attributes th[e] Members of a Body to it: *Who shall deliver m[e] from the Body of Sin and Death?* &c. And in an[-] other Place he positively calls *Fornication, Unclean[-] ness, inordinate Affections, evil Concupiscence, a[nd] Covetousness*, &c. Members of this Body: Besid[es] What is that *Old-Man* which he speaks of else[-] where, and stirs up the Godly to put off, but *Sin* or the evil Habits thereof, which are corrupt, a[c-] *cording to the deceitful Lusts*.

Now, that we may the better perform thi[s] great and profitable Work we have taken in Han[d], it will be needful first of all, to discover the *P[e-] digree, Rise, Antiquity*, and *Original* of this abo[-] minable Enemy of all Mankind.

First, *Negatively*; 'Tis evident *Sin* is not of no[r] from God: He that is Holiness and Goodness it[-] self, cannot be the Author directly nor indirect[ly] of *Sin or Ungodliness*. *A good Tree cannot bring fo[rth] evil Fruit*; from whomsoever therefore *Sin* deriv[ed] his first Being, or had his Original, it is impossi[-] ble he should be from the Glorious Creator [of] Heaven and Earth; for whatsoever God creat[ed] was Good: Every Thing that had its Being f[rom] him hath some Good originally in it; but *Sin* hath not, nor never had any Good in it, but is altogether Evil, the Evil of Evils; and therefore not from God.

Yet we must grant that *Sin* is of great Antiquity, and hath been a long Time in the World; yea, some there be who think he had his Conception or Original before Man was created, because some of the Angels (as they conceive) were overcome, and fell by him before that Time; but how, where, and by what Means *Sin* entered into them, who were such Holy and Glorious Creatures considered in their first Estate, is, as I judge, beyond what any Mortal is able to demonstrate; therefore we shall state his Original where the Apostle doth: *By one Man Sin entered into the World*; that is to say, *Sin* was conceived, and had his Birth or Entrance into this World by Means of our first Parents; but if it be asked, by whom he was begotten; I answer, By *Apollyon*, King of the Bottomless Pit, called the Old Serpent, the Devil and Satan: It was by his Subtilty they were beguiled, who whilst they stood in the State of Innocency, were as a most chaste, beautiful and undefiled Virgin, whom because he could not force, he cunningly enticed to his foul and unclean Embraces; yea, and upon their first yielding to this cursed Serpent, was begotten this vile and evil Enemy: Hence the Devil is said to be *a Liar, and the Father of it*; and upon this Account, *Sin* may be fitly called *the Spawn of the Devil*: 'Tis originally his Offspring, a Brat of his getting; and also bears a lively Image and Resemblance of him.

A 5 *Object.*

Object. But this you will say was the Original or First *Sin*.

Answ. 'Tis true, and must also be granted, That that *Original Sin*, was the Original of all *Sins*; for from that First Sin, and by the Help of the Devil, and Man's evil Heart, doth all Manner of *Sin* proceed.

Original Sin hath been prodigious fruitful; for it would make a Man admire to consider what a Multitude of filthy *Brats*, or spurious *Offspring* have proceeded from that First-born of the Devil; yet all are but as it were Members or Parts of, and tend to make up the said Body and evil Monster: And this truly, of the Production of *Sin*, was *Apollyon*'s Master-Piece; for by the Help and Means thereof, he hoped and resolved to erect his Kingdom: For since he could not be a Ruler (nor in a higher State than a Servant) in the Upper World; (no, nor remain an Angel any longer there) he was resolved to be a King and Ruler in these lower Regions, and to set up a mighty Kingdom in this World in despight of God himself; whom he sought thereby to be revenged upon, for that great Affront and Indignity cast upon him (as 'tis thought) he conceived, who being created in a higher and more glorious State than Man, should be commanded to be a Servant or Ministring Spirit to Man; and he was, doubtless, moved also with Malice and Rage against the Creature Man, whom he saw God had lately formed and placed in Paradise, and made Lord and chief Ruler of the Universe. And to the End that he might, I say, effect or bring this his grand Plot or Enterprize about, which was to eclipse God's Glory, and utterly

Mankind, he saw there was no other Way to accomplish it, but by the Production of this cruel and merciless Enemy, *Sin*; and having craftily obtained his devilish Design, so far that the Hellish Monster was conceived and brought forth, immediately as soon as ever he had entered into the World, even before he was one Hour old, he began to act his Diabolical, Cursed and Damnable Pranks; so that by his first Essay or Entrance on his fearful Work or Enterprize, he gave sufficient Proof to all that should ever live on Earth, of his Strength and Cruelty, and what all Mortals must expect from him. 'Tis strange to consider, that a *Brat* just born, and as one would think, wholly unexperienced, should be cloathed with so much Power, and be filled with so great Malice; for just as *Apollyon* Midwiv'd him into the World, he let fly his *Sting*, and thereby at once gave a mortal Wound to the whole Lump of Mankind; not only to all that Then lived, but also to such who should in After-times live upon the Earth. The Nature of that woeful Blow, it may not be amiss if I further open and explain, before I proceed; since we all to this Day feel it, and groan under the sad Misery and dreadful Effects thereof.

But e'er I do this, let it be observed, That *Sin* at once in a great Measure, did effect what *Apollyon* craftily, in both Respects, had purposed before to ing about. For hereby he caused Man to cast ff his ever Blessed and Glorious Sovereign, from whom he had his Breath and Being; nay, not only so, but he begat a Strangeness, and irreconcileable Enmity in the Heart of Man to the ever Blessed God, which is a most dismal Thing to consider

sider of; neither could any other Enemy ever have done this evil and cursed Deed, but *Sin* only. Nay, and as he made Man to become God's Enemy, so he also caused God to become an Enemy to Man; (there being nothing so hateful and contrary to his pure and holy Nature, than *Sin*,) insomuch that now that Blessed Union that was between God the Holy Creator, and Man his once happy Creature, is broke.

So that from hence you may see, This Enemy flew, as soon as ever he was born, into the very Face of God himself: This was his great Cry then, and is still to this Day, *God shall not Reign, but I will Reign; and Apollyon King of Darkness, he shall Reign, and Rule in the Hearts of all Men on Earth.* Moreover, that by that one Act, he most wickedly defaced God's Glorious Image, which was graciously stamped upon the Soul of Man; and basely corrupted those noble Faculties, who, as I may say, were the Attendants, Bosom Friends, and continual Companions of this High-born Soul, whose Names were (if I mistake not) these following, viz.

1. *Judgment*, alias *Understanding*, a very Grave and Wise Counsellor; but now become Blind, filled with *Incredulity* and *Enmity*.

2. *Will*, a Free and Loyal Friend to the King of Heaven and Earth; and one always ready to stir up this precious Soul to that which was for her Good, and her Sovereign's Interest; until he was by this Enemy depraved, and wretchedly corrupted, being wholly brought over to promote the Interest of *Apollyon*. Neither is there in any a greater Perverseness to the Will of God; for being filled

with Pride, he ever seeks to exalt himself, and all who adhere to him, above God, his Holy Word, and Glorious Sovereignty.

3. *Memory*, who before continually put the Soul in Mind of all Things God had commanded her to do, and whatsoever he had prohibited or enjoined her not to do; but now so corrupted by this Enemy, and made so vile, that what she should remember, she forgets; and what she should forget, that she remembers.

4. *Affections*: And indeed there were none more basely changed, and drawn away from God, than these; Before *Sin* prevailed, or entered into the World, they were like a most chaste and undefiled Virgin; but now so corrupted and carnal, that they are more disordered than any of the rest: Before they were always set upon God, and took up Delight and Complacency in Him, He being their only *Object*: But Now the *World*, the *Flesh*, nay, this Hell-bred Tyrant, *Sin*, is Sweeter, more Precious and Lovely to them than He.

5. *Conscience*: One who kept the *Records*, was always faithful to the Soul before the unhappy Prolapsion of this Enemy of God, and made all the House to rejoice and break forth into singing, by the Nature of his sweet Testimony, or Witness, he always gave in, for, and in Behalf of the Soul; but now so vile and depraved, that when he should reprove and charge the Soul with its Evils, he is asleep; sometimes he condemns for want of good Eye-sight, when he should justify; and at another Time justifies when he should reprove and condemn. Nay, he is so far drawn aside to the Interest of the Prince of Darkness, that when some

Men

Men persecute, and put the Saints of God to Death, he tells them they do God Service. These are some of those Things that this vile Enemy did in part effect, by that one Blow he struck our First Parents, tho' not all; for he brought in, or did beget another most cruel Tyrant, who hath reigned ever since with great Force and Rigour, subduing all under his Feet; his Name is *Death*. This King of Terror had never been, had not *Sin* given his Being to him: In a Word, You may perceive he became an immediate Plague to the Soul of Man, a Depriver of every Faculty, and a Destroyer of the Body. For it was he also who let in Sickness, and all Manner of Diseases which the Bodies of all human Creatures are now subject to.

Lastly, *Hell*, or the *Lake of Fire* comes to be prepared by his Means: 'Tis he, I mean, who brings in *Eternal Death*. There had been no *Hell*, had it not been for *Sin*.

Sin's worse than Hell: it digg'd that horrid Pit,
'Tis Sin that casts poor Sinners into it;
No Lake of Fire, no Tophet had there been
For Souls of Men; no Death, but through Sin.

CHAP. II.

Shewing how Apollyon, *Prince of Darkness, having a Design to send* Tyrant Sin *as his grand Agent, to Travel into all Quarters of the Earth; he* (First) *Gave him his Commission. Secondly, Warning of his Enemies. Thirdly, Directions how to Overcome and Destroy them.*

THE Pedigree, Rise, Original, and Antiquity of this cruel and Hell-bred Enemy, *Sin*, having

having briefly been opened to you: *Apollyon* having now nourished and brought him up fit for his Turn, Work, and Service, and finding he had already so wonderfully succeeded in his first and main Enterprize, he saw he would be a true and faithful Friend to him, and a rare Foot-stool or Stirrup for him, to mount or raise him up to his longed-for Sovereignty; and finding him by this Time grown to some considerable Maturity, resolved to send him Abroad to Travel into all Quarters of the Earth, to manage the Affairs of his Infernal Kingdom, greaten his Power, and actually subdue all Enemies under his Feet, in all Nations, Countries, and Kingdoms of the World. But before the Tyrant entered upon this woeful Journey, we will suppose the Devil gave him his Commission and Instructions how to proceed in all his Atchievements; to whom he addressed himself after this Manner:

My most dear and beloved Child, the true Image of thy Father, and choice Darling of Hell, and the only Hope of this Infernal Lake, whom my Lord *Lucifer*, *Belzebub*, and other inferior Princes, as *Belial*, *Sathan*, &c. do adore; hearken to thy Father, who begat thee, and gave thy Being to thee: Thou art my Creature: What care I tho' the Powers of Heaven hate thee? I will, in despite of all thy mortal Enemies, make thee Great, raise thy Honours, and crown thee as King and chief Ruler throughout the whole Universe; and all who will not obey thee, and yield Subjection to thee, I will raise all Manner of Mischief upon, make them miserable, and tread them under thy Feet. Thou seest how successful already thou hast been, and what a mighty Conqueror thou art become in thy

thy very Non-age. Thou hast at one Blow, defeated all the Hopes of this new born Mortal, and crushed him to Pieces in the very Bud. He that was the other Day the Darling of Heaven, who swam in Pleasures, and was mounted so high in Sovereignty, Glory, and inconceivable Grandeur, shining as a Star of the first Magnitude, possessing perfect Union and Communion with his Creator, is now by thee, by the Power of thy Hand, and Success of thy Arms, made miserable, and become so hateful to him whose Delight he was, that he hath cast him off, and turned him out of Paradise. Ah, how I laugh to see it! How is he become the Reproach and Scorn of all the Princes and mighty Host of this unconquered Lake! What care I, tho' there is much bitter Enmity put between me and the *Woman's Seed*? Do I fear what Hurt any one that shall proceed from Her can do to me? If thou in thy Non-age hast done such mighty Things, and overcome this Excellent Creature, when all his internal Powers were utterly averse to us, and no ways inclined to favour our Interest; what can any of her Offspring do to our Hurt, much less *break my Head*, or destroy thy Sovereignty, since now we have got so strong a Party on our Side, in their own House? Thou hast been so happy in this late mighty Victory, that the Powers of that noble Soul, possessed by this Creature, are at once brought over to Us.

I have a Purpose to send thee to Travel to and fro in the Earth, until thou hast gone through the whole Universe: And, to my Joy, I find all People are prepared for thee, and made willing to receive thee; for all their Faculties seem inclined to

The Travels of Ungodliness. 17

tertain thee, so that I have no Cause to doubt
an happy Progress. I am sure thou wilt find
ready Welcome in all Places, not only amongst
the Poor, and Baser Sort, but amongst the Mighty
and Noble Ones of the Earth.

And now therefore know that I am thy Prince
and only Sovereign; and I do here
give thee a Commission, a Passport *Apollyon*
ready drawn, and signed for thee *gives Pecca-*
by all the High and Mighty Lords *tum, or Sin,*
of these dark and vast Regions; *his Commission.*
with certain Instructions how to carry thyself in
all thy Travels. I have also prepared for thee two
great Wings, that sometimes (as Need shall require) thou mayest fly to and fro, and be as swift as
Thought: The vast Deep shall be no Lett to thee;
thou shalt pass from Port to Port, from Place to
Place, from one Land and Kingdom to another,
without Ship or Galley, and shall never need to
stay for Wind or Tide: I will also teach thee to
transform thyself into any Form or Shape at my
Pleasure; and to hide thy Sting and ugly Visage,
I have provided thee a Cloak, which thou shalt
have Power and Skill to alter, or change the Fashion of as will best suit thy Occasion at any Time.
Be thou sometimes a Dog to fawn; a Dragon to
devour; a Dove to seem innocent; be a Serpent,
Fox or Subtilty; a Lyon for Strength; and in
thy Travels, observe the Constitutions and natural Inclinations of all People: Build rather thy
Nest amongst Willows that bend every Way, than
the Tops of Oaks, whose Heads are hard to be
broken. Fly with the Swallow close to the Earth,
when Storms are at hand; but keep Company
with

with Birds of greater Talons when the Weath[er]
is clear, and never leave them till they look lik[e]
Ravens. Creep into every Bosom; fear not t[o]
approach the Courts of Emperors, Kings, Princes,
and Noble Ones of the Earth; for I will cau[se]
thee to find Favour amongst all Ranks, Degree[s]
and Conditions of Men. I will teach thee to g[et]
in at their Eyes, Ears and Mouth; nay, a Thousan[d]
Ways thou shalt have to invade them; and t[o]
spread the Wings of thy Infection over them, mak[e]
every Head thy Pillow to lean upon; and use [it]
like a Mill, to grind Mischief. When thou meet[-]
est a *Dutchman*, teach him to Drink; wher wit[h]
a *Frenchman*, teach him to Stab; when a *Span[i]-*
ard, how to betray; present an *Italian* with a fa[ir]
Damsel, and teach him to Poison; when tho[u]
meetest a *Scot*, teach him False-heartedness; wh[en]
with an *Irishman*, teach him to forswear himsel[f];
when an *Englishman*, to do all this: Pursue Gre[at]
Men hard; they are my very good Benefactors
and their Example hath commonly a great Influence upon those of a lower Rank. Haunt T[a]-
verns, there thou shalt find brave Youths easi[ly]
overcome. Erect Store of Play-Houses, or th[ey]
tend greatly to the enlarging of my Principalities
there I keep my Market, and vend my Ware m[ost]
abundantly, or offer my rotten Goods to Sale, bu[r]-
nished up bravely to the Eye, enough to bewit[ch]
all who lack Understanding, to dote upon then[.]

Be sure to beset (on every Side) the Young
Sort; for if thou canst get Possession of th[eir]
Hearts timely, thou wilt find it easy to keep th[em]
safe enough, and make them thy constant Sla[ves]
and Vassals to the End. And when thou mee[test]

The Travels of Ungodliness. 19

...th them afterwards, shew them the Glory of ...his World, allure them with thy Pleasures, and ...old forth thy Golden Apples to them: But if ...hat sorry Fellow, *Conscience*, at any Time, gets ...Power to frighten them, promise them *Late Repentance*, and assure them of *Long Life*; and there...y thou wilt soon overcome them.

When thou meetest with the *Rich*, tempt them ...o trust in it, set their Hearts upon it, and to make ...their Bags of *Gold* and *Silver* their *God*; and to ...grind the Face of the *Poor*, and force them to sell ...their Commodities cheaper than they can afford ...them, and not give them a Penny to relieve their ...Necessities: For thereby thou wilt subdue them ...oth at once; for the one I am sure of, and the ...her will be so hunted with one of thy Offspring, ...lled *Carping Care*, that if *Light-Fingers* doth not ...vercome and tempt him to Steal, the other will ...reak his Heart, and force him to take the Name ...f God in vain, and not think of any thing else, ...han what will tend to the strengthening of thy ...nds, and conduce to my Interest in him.

When thou comest to meet with such who are ...rally inclined to Ambition, or have an eager ...re and Thirst after Honour, suit thy Bait ac...ngly; teach them how to contemn their God, ...Conscience, their Good Name, the Law and ...ion too, that so they may the better mount ...ill of *Ambition* and *Earthly Grandeur*.

...hen thou dost approach to a melancholy Per... ...ntice him to be alone, and not to open his ...to any Body, as he values his Life: Also ...de him, no Body in the World can tell what ...stemper is; and to make him believe he is
damned:

20   The Progress of SIN: Or,

damned: Nay, tell him there is no Way, but
Hell he must go; and then we shall between us,
perhaps, entice him to hang, drown, or poison
himself, or cut his own Throat; and so we shall
destroy many of these silly Souls, and that Way
enlarge our Kingdom.

When thou meetest with an Old Man, make
him conceited, vain-glorious, fretful, and very
peevish; fill his Head with Tales and old Stories;
and to put them off the better, tempt him to add
to them.

When thou comest to Married People, make
one Jealous of the other: If a Man have a beautiful Woman to his Wife, trouble his Thoughts
without just Cause; because she is fair, make him
conclude she is false, and every one that looks on
her, persuade him, loves her. If she speaketh him
fair, let him believe she feigneth; if she behave
herself dutiful, make him think she then doth
counterfeit. When she goes Abroad, fill his Head
with Fear, and make his Heart pant. If she be
neatly dressed, persuade him 'tis to allure and
please others. If she be homely dressed, 'tis because she knows that he will keep House that Day.
If by any Means we can but kindle this Spark
either of them, to be jealous-headed, we shall
our Business effectually.

Be sure do what you can to make Discord
tween every Couple; when one is hot, let not
other be cold; suffer not one to throw Water
on the Fire which the other kindles; for by
Means we shall set the House on Fire, and
warm ourselves with the Heat thereof. T
them to live either below what they have,

... what they have; and if they have Children, I ... ill give thee Instructions about them hereafter, ... en thou enterest the Country of *Non-age*: If ... y go behind-hand, thou must stir up the Hus— ... d to lay all the Cause thereof on his Wife, ... let the Wife charge the Husband wholly with ... Do what thou canst, be sure, in the Morning ... d Evening, to prevent *Prayer*; for that I fear ... ore than all the *Pope's Holy Water*.

We must make the Fountain muddy, and then ... Spring cannot be clear: Discord and Confusion ... a Family, does as much strengthen my King— ... n as any Thing in the World. You cannot ... k how I am pleased, how greatly it delights ... to see Men and their Wives live at Strife and ... ance.

... hen thou meetest with a Single, or Un-mar— ... Person, perplex his Mind continually about a ... , and render his Life not worth Regard with— ... ne: If thou canst tempt him to Uncleanness, ... I will stand his Friend in the Matter: But if ... ill Marry, let him more mind the Portion ... the Person; let his Enquiry be what Money ... hath, not what Grace she hath, as you love ... We must also find out such an one for him ... ay be a Plague to him, as *Job's* Wife was to ... Never let him mind the Temper of the Wo— ... nor whether she will or no be a suitable ... meet, so that she doth but please his Eye, and ... Store of Gold and Silver into his Coffer.

... en thou dost assault a cholerick or passionate ... raise his Anger to Madness; if thou canst, ... his Mind to swell high, and so full, that there ... e no room left for any good Word or Motion.

Make

Make him in his Fits like a *Spider-poison'd Toad*; that *Reason, Modesty, Peace* and *Humanity* may fl[y] from him, as People do from a House that is all o[n] Fire; let it be contumely, without any Distincti[on] or Respect had to Friend or Foe, Alliant or Fam[i]liar; let him also add Violence of Hands, sava[ge] or monstrous Behaviour, like the troubled Sea wh[en] it cannot rest; whose Waters cast up Mire an[d] Dirt, fuming and foaming like a muddy Channel, a distorted Countenance, sparkling Eyes, foul Language, and let him not come to himself, nor spea[k] a Word to his nearest Friends for two or thre[e] Days; nay, stir him up in his mad Fit to r[un] away, tho' there was no Cause for the Fuel; a[nd] if thou canst, persuade him to throw the *House at Window*, tear his Wife's Linen and fine Cloa[ths] to Pieces, or break her Earthen Ware. But kn[ow] we are curious Observers of the Tempers and [va]rious Passions of Men; in some Anger-hat[h] quick and sudden Motion, but presently cea[se.] This they call *Choler*; and they think it is an [In]fluence of some angry *Planet*: Let the Fools h[ave] their Fancy; but I must tell thee, 'tis a Chil[d of] thy begetting; but this is like *Fire in Stubble*, s[oon] *kindled*, and soon *goes out*; or like *Gun-pow*[der,] which no sooner thou puttest Fire to, but it [flies] in the Faces of their dearest Friends. These t[hey] say are the best-natured Men; but they may th[ank] us for that Excuse.

There is another Sort whom thou canst n[ot] suddenly move; but when Passion is raised, it [takes] deeper hold in their Memory: And as this F[ire is] not so easily kindled, so neither is it easily put [out.] If thou dost but do thy best, 'twill prove like F[ire in] Iron, which hardly taketh, and long abideth.

A Third Sort there be, in whom thou may'st
[kin]dle this fiery Passion suddenly, and retain it
[pe]rpetually; not desisting without Revenge. These
[are] like Fire, which ceaseth not without the Ruin
[and] Waste of that Matter whereon it hath caught.
[Mi]nd thy Instructions; for by this Engine thou
[m]ay'st destroy Thousands.

There is yet another kind of People which thou
must attack, whom I perfectly hate, and hold for
my mortal Enemies; and they are called *Saints*,
about whom we have held divers Grand Councils
[in] Hell, how to destroy. These are they who are
[s]tiled the *Woman's Seed*.

Most Noble Prince, If thou canst beguile, de-
[ceiv]e and subdue this Sort, the Day is our own.
[Tho]u must do it, or it can never be done. There-
[fore] I conjure thee, in the Name of my Lord *Lucifer*, *Belzebub*, and in the Name of all the Mighty
[Th]rones, *Dominions*, *Principalities*, and *Powers* of
[th]is *Burning Lake*, to use thy utmost Skill and Po-
[lic]y; for what thou doest upon these, thou must
[d]o by Craft, and after a more wary and clande-
[stin]e Manner; for they have studied our *Politicks*,
[and] are *not ignorant of our Devices*. Yet let me
[tel]l thee, there are some who bear that Name,
[an]d are accounted of their Company, who are
[our] good Friends, and indeed as serviceable to our
[Int]erest, as most in the World.

But as touching *Advice* and *Counsel*, how thou
[shou]ld'st prey upon those my grand Enemies, I
[mu]st forbear at present, it being a Secret that ought
[not t]o be revealed: I shall give thee therefore In-
[struct]ions hereafter, when thou meetest with them
[in the] *Town of Religion*, how to betray and over-
[come] them.   More-

24 *The* Progress *of* SIN: *Or*,

Moreover, there are divers other Ranks, Qu[a]lities and Conditions of People, with whom t[hou] wilt meet in thy Travels, which I have not [yet] mentioned, *viz. Noblemen, Counsellors, La[w]wy[ers], Doctors,* &c. and all Sorts of *Mechanicks*. [But] when thou enterest into the Town of *Comm[on]*, thou shalt have Advice and Directions how [to] handle them.

And now, because I am sensible of the great Weight and Importance of this grand Enterprize, and how by thy Travels I am like to lose or wi[n] all; I am resolved to accompany thee contin[ually] to the End of the World. I will go with t[hee] and be as a Servant to thee. And I must tell [thee] also, I have got the Skill to transform myself [into] any Shape: If need be, I can be an *Angel of L[ight]* and become Devilish Godly: We must both [some]times be v[ery] Religious; for else, how shoul[d we] set up our Spiritual Kingdom; for such g[od we] have, and shall have, as well as a Fleshly. A[nd] the Advantage thereby to us is, and will be, v[ery] great; otherwise we should never have spent [so] much Time, and held so many grand Caba[ls in] Hell, about contriving, ushering in, and esta[blish]ing this our Ecclesiastical State in the World.

Lastly, That we may not lose Time, I shall [now] admonish thee of divers grand Enemies which [thou] must be aware of, and thoroughly revenged u[pon,] or all our Design will prove in a great Me[asure] fruitless: I shall therefore, e'er thou beg[in thy] Travels, give thee their Names.

The First is a *Paper-Enemy*, a contempti[ble one] to look upon, and yet I dread him more t[han] the Powers of Heaven and Earth. May i[t]

The Travels *of* Ungodliness.   25

...se your Greatness, 'tis a Book; not a Play-
...k; No, no, that is an Engine of my own
...ing: Not a Conjuring-Book; for that same
...ing hath often made me brave Sport; Nor is it
...ing-Book; No, nor a Book of Philosophy, nor
...sick: But 'tis the *Bible*. I could wish all the
Plagues of Hell to light upon it, if that would do;
but I see all is in vain, for 'tis under the perpetual
Care of *Him* who reigns Above, and did cast me
down into these Lower Regions. We must therefore do what we can to keep all Men ignorant of
it, and not suffer them to have it in their *Mother-
Tongue*: Or, if we cannot do that, then take off
their Hearts from it so that they may not read, me-
ditate upon it, nor remember what is contained in
it; for 'tis like a cruel Sword with two Edges,
which if they have got Skill to use, it will destroy
thee utterly. Yet do not fear; for I can teach
thee so to use it, as to turn the Edge of it against
themselves, and wound them with their own
Weapons. Besides, I will shew thee how to mag-
...fy some other Books, and unwritten Verities,
...eer Inventions of our own devising, above it;
and raise up others to cast it away as a dead Letter,
and also to wrest it, and to make a Nose of Wax
of it, and cause Thousands to believe that it doth
not belong to Lay-People to read it, and forewarn
them not to study it, on their Perils.

  The Second Enemy I must advise thee of, is one
Theology, a *Holder-forth*, a *Preacher* forsooth, that
...es himself up wholly to study how to bring both
...e and I to Shame; nay, and to destroy Thee ut-
...y. This Fellow pryes into all our Secrets; but
...ll teach thee how, one Way or other, to be re-
...ed upon him.   B   The

The Third Adversary is a Spirit, some call the *Holy Spirit*. I must confess he is a powe[rful] Enemy, and I cannot deny but that he hath b[een] sometimes too hard for all the mighty Power[s of] this Burning Lake. Whensoever therefore [he] breaks in upon thee, with his Sword drawn in [his] Hand, he will slay thee at once. Nay, such cr[uel] Hatred he hath to thee, that no other Death wil[l] satisfy him but to crucify thee, which grieves my Heart to think upon. Therefore beware of him, and keep the Door shut (where thou hast Possession) against him. Moreover, I shall teach thee many other Ways to quench his Hea[t], and hinder his prevailing Power upon Mens Hearts; yea, tire his Patience, and grieve him so, that he shall not strive against thee, nor appear for their Help any longer.

The Fourth is a rare and beautiful Damsel, her Name is *Grace*; and she hath also several Sisters, as *Faith*, *Hope*, *Charity*, &c. It grieves me to think thou shouldest at any Time be worsted, and utterly vanquished by any of the *Feminine Gender*[.] But thou wilt sustain great Loss, I perceive, b[y] her Means; for she has a cruel Train of power[ful] Enemies to torment us, continually attending on her; yet I shall teach thee how to marr her Beauty, and spoil her Growth.

The Fifth Enemy is called *Knowledge of God*; but I think there is no great Fear of him; for the greatest Part of the World, I doubt not, but we shall keep in *Ignorance*, in *Heathenish* and *Popish Darkness*: But if he gets in, he will do us gre[at] Hurt, by discovering all our Intrigues.

The Sixth is only *Morality*: I hate him as a M[an] hates a Toad. Yet, as we will order Matters,

The Travels of Ungodliness.

...do us a great Kindness; for he is not very ...known, and so we will cause divers silly Crea...es to trust in him for Life and Salvation. That ...ay we shall bring some solid Blades to Hell, with ...e Hopes of Heaven in their Noddles.

The Seventh is a scurvy, obstinate Fellow, cal... *Enlightned Conscience*; a meer Tell-tale; one ...never will be bribed, nor doth he fear Frowns, ...regard Flatteries. I doubt he will prove a ...gue to thee in all thy Travels: but I will shew ...e hereafter how to deal with him.

The Eighth is an Engine of War; an Enemy that has made the very Foundations of Hell itself to shake; I think they call him *Prayer*; but he can do little Hurt without *Faith*; and I will teach thee many rare Devices to make him ineffectual. There are some *Prayers* thou need'st not fear, viz. such that some use with *Beads*, &c. Prayer always prevails according to the *Nature*, *Holiness*, *Truth*, *Sincerity*, *Fervency*, *Skill*, and *Care* of the Person who uses Him.

The Ninth is *Repentance*; but fear him not if he comes not in timely, or approaches alone without his dreadful Retinue, whom I tremble at the Thoughts of; which are these following, viz. *Godly-Sorrow*, *Holy-Revenge*, *Vehement-Desire*, *Spiritual-Indignation*, *Filial-Fear*, *Heavenly-Care*, *Self-Clearing*, *Fiery-Zeal*, &c.

The Tenth Enemy is *Consideration*, who is the ...ngleader to all the *Mischiefs*, *Troubles*, *Wars* and ...*quietments* raised up in any *Kingdom*; and were ...ot for him, I would not fear any Adversary on ...th; therefore thou must prevent his coming to ...Assistance of the Parties thou dost encounter

with,

28   *The Progress of* SIN: Or,

with, which thou mayest do by filling their Mi[nds]
with the Cares of this Life; also render him o[di]‑
ous, make them believe he is a dangerous Fello[w,]
hath made many a brisk Youngster a meer Dro[ne,]
causing them to hang down their Heads like B[ul]‑
rushes, to fold their Arms, and to spend their D[ays]
in Tears and Sighing, and hath caused many to [be]
besides themselves. Moreover, thou mayest dr[ive]
him away, by sending the Party to some *Play,*
Tavern, or such like Diversion.

The Eleventh are, *Truth* and *Justice,* both i[m]‑
placable Enemies to our Empire; but I am r[e]‑
solved to make them wander like *Vagabonds* in t[he]
open Air; for *Truth* shall find no Lodging, unles[s]
it be with a *Mute*; and *Justice,* thou shalt throw
her down in the Streets, and *Equity* shall not enter.
We will so handle her, that few or none shall
know her when they see her: They shall indeed
have her bare Name, but not her Nature; for I
have ready at hand in every Kingdom, a Multi‑
tude of such brave *Cut-holes,* that I hope they
effectually will do her Business. Let her fly to
Heaven, what hath she to do on Earth? And as
for her who bears that Name, we will turn her
Sword against our Enemies (and as much as in us
lies) to spare our Friends.

The Twelfth Enemy is, one whom they call
The Gospel, who hath been Travelling up and
down a long Time, to undermine my Kingdom.
He is made up, men say, with a *right Faith,* a[nd]
holy Life; but I am glad he meets with no bett[er]
Entertainment. Now, my grand Design by gra[nt]‑
ing thee this Commission, is to spoil his Enter‑
prize, and finally, to vanquish him out of the [fol]‑
low

lower Regions. Ponder well what hath been said, and bestir yourself: Fly to and fro, *East*, *West*, *North* and *South*, beset all Mortals; my Instructions will serve for every Age, and will suit with all Climates and Countries throughout the whole Universe; but chiefly I aim at the latter Times. Be gone, and raise my Honour, and let my Renown break forth in all Quarters.

Cloath my ambitious Children with Ornaments of Gold, and crown them with Glory and Honour; fill the Voluptuous with Pleasure, and all the Delights of this World. Let the Envious and Cholerick have all the sweet Revenge their Hearts can desire; glut them with Rapine, Massacre and Murder. Set one Man against another; Husband against the Wife, the Wife against the Husband; Parents against the Children, and Children against their Parents; and teach Masters to be cruel to their Servants, and Servants to rob and steal from their Masters; promoting *Lying, Swearing, Whoring, Blasphemy, Atheism, Flattery, Drunkenness, Cruelty, Pride, Hard heartedness*, and all Manner of *Debauchery*. Raise up Wars and Commotions in every Kingdom; let all before thee be put to Fire and Sword. Introduce Superstition, Heresy, False Doctrine, and gross Idolatry. Visit all in thy Journey; the Young, the Old, the High, the Low, the Rich, the Poor, the King on the Throne, the Beggar on the Dunghill. Let Truth, Righteousness, Justice, and Equity, Conscience, Charity, Fidelity, Simplicity and Modesty, be banished all the Regions of the Earth. Thou art my great Agent, and hast thy Patent of Assignment and Grant from me the great *Prince of Darkness*, whom thou dost daily honour, and under whose Standard continually advance thy Colours, and spread the Flag of my Authority; by which, not only the Lodges and outward Gates of all Courts and Cities of the World, but also the inward and inmost Closets and Chambers therein, will soon fly open, and give way to this strong Commission. Thou hast the World, the Flesh, and Me the Devil; nay, all Devils and Infernal Spirits for thee, to side with thee, and take thy Part. All Men are ready to receive thee; no Tradesmen nor others can well live without thee; but be sure remember thou never be satisfied to take up thy Quarters in their Barns nor Stables, nor in their outward Courts nor Castle-Yards; but command the best Room they have, viz. their Hearts; and be sure where thou comest to sway the Scepter, and make them all subject to thee, and become thy Servants and Vassals for ever. Let me see thee bring Millions of Millions into these dark Regions, to dwell with us in Everlasting Burnings.

CHAP. III.

Shewing how the haughty Prince and bloody Tyrant Sin, the grand Agent of Apollyon, *began his Travels: Also what a strange Retinue doth accompany him; and his great Success in the Beginning of his actual Enterprize.*

THIS Hellish Monster, having thus received his Commission, immediately resolved (as you may conclude) for his Journey. But

But before we come to speak of his present Travels, it is necessary to give you a Description of his Person and Retinue; together, with a brief History of his first Setting out, and abominable Transactions in ancient Times.

First, As to his Person, he is the strangest Monster that ever you heard or read of; for he consists of a compleat Composition of all manner of Sins and Ungodliness; and tho' he be but one entire Body, yet he hath a Multitude of Members, and lives separately in every one of them; so that each Member may properly be said to be him, as if he was solely or entirely there. 'Tis not proper to say he is a *Sinner,* for he is got into a higher Orb than that Phrase can reach; not filthy, but Filthiness in the Abstract; not proud, but Pride; not covetous, but Covetousness, and so forth.

Secondly, He being in the Holy Scripture compared to a mighty King, tho' a cruel Tyrant, whose Power and Authority is very great; it will do well to shew you what a Retinue he always hath to accompany him in his Progress; for it cannot be supposed he Travels alone. The 1st is, *Apollyon,* King of the *Bottomless Pit.* 2. *Intolerable Guilt.* 3. *Abominable Pollution.* 4. *Horrible Shame* and *Ignominy.* 5. *Deceitful Heart.* 6. *Defiled Conscience.* 7. *Famine.* 8. *The Sword.* 9. *Pestilence.* 10. *Death,* who is always just at his Heels; and *Hell,* with the dreadful Wrath and Curse of an angry God, pursues him very close, from which there is no escaping.

Moreover, The rich Presents the Traveller carries along with him, to allure, entice, or ensnare the Souls of Men, are chiefly *Sinful Pleasures, Riches,*

Riches, Honours, and *Length of Days.* But stop here! *Apollyon* is near, and seems to be in a great Rage that his Agent is not gone.

Apol. Haste, thou mighty Champion, prepare for thy Journey; subdue the World actually under thy Feet; fear no Enemy that seeks to undermine or counter-work thee. I like no Delays; lose no Time; put the Mandates of thy Sovereign into present Execution, before I raise all the Power of this unconquered Lake upon my Enemies, and consume all Mortals at once.

Upon which the cruel Enemy set forth, *Apollyon* following him close at his Heels, to assist him in every Enterprize: And so it fell out, just as he began his Journey, *Cain* and *Abel* were offering Sacrifices; and having Intelligence of both their Dispositions, he made up to *Cain*'s Door, and there lay couching down, like a hurtful Beast, ready to devour, and secretly whispered into his Ear, *To spare the best of his Substance to enrich himself*; and also intimated to him, *That all he offered to the Lord was lost, and would never be rewarded*; and *Faith* not being in *Cain*'s House, he hearkened to this cursed Stranger, and did accordingly; yet he brought his Offering, lest he should displease his Father *Adam*, who, it is thought, at that Time was High-Priest, which Office afterwards fell to the First-born in the Family. But when *Cain* saw his Offering was not accepted, and his Brother's was, this Enemy being near, knocked at his Door.

Cain. Who is there?

Sin. Have you, Sir, any Room for a Traveller?

Cain. What are you?

Sin. A Friend; one that loves you dearly, and am troubled

troubled to see how you are abused, and basely dealt with by your younger Brother. Can you bear the Thoughts that he should be in the Favour of his Maker, and the only Darling of his Father, and you slighted and despised in this Sort?

Cain. By this I cannot but think thou art indeed a Friend, and bearest Good-will to me; pray come in.

And he presently lodged him in the best Room he had; neither do I read of any Opposition made against him by any in the House.

He had no sooner received him, but immediately (by secret Instigations and Instructions from *Apollyon*, who was glad to see him entertained) he applied himself to him in this Manner:

Sin. Let this Villain *Abel* be the Object of thy Hatred: Never speak friendly to him more in Love, but let thy Wrath out against him to the uttermost. Shall he be accepted? What's he? Art thou not better than he? He will e'er long (tho' thy younger Brother) become thy Lord and Master, and Ruler over thee; and thou shalt be made a meer Underling.

Cain. I am truly of your Mind; my Father and Mother's Heart, I find is already taken from me, and set upon this cunning Supplanter. I hate him with a perfect Hatred; neither can I endure to see him.

Thus *Cain* was filled with Wrath, and his Countenance fell; that is, he shewed himself full of Rage and Discontent.

Sin. Most Noble *Cain*, Heir of the World; I have a Business of great Importance to impart to thee.

Cain. Sir, what is it?

Sin. I am a Servant to a mighty Prince, whose Power and Kingdom, 'tis like thou hast not heard of: And he hath a dear and cordial Love for thee, and hath sent me to thee with certain Instructions, to put thee in a Way how to be rid of this canting Brother; and I will assure you, 'tis high Time, for he is now at Prayer, and begins to grow more and more in Favour.

Cain. I am glad to hear this News: But which Way can the Thing be done?

Sin. Sir, you will never be at Peace, nor have any Ground to conclude your Father will make you his Heir, or indeed ever regard you, till he be rid out of the World: But if this be once done, all is your own.

Cain. But how shall I do to get rid of him?

Sin. Why, since there is none you can employ secretly to do it; do you kill him, and then declare he murdered himself, being overcome with Melancholy, or blown up with Pride and Self-conceit upon his late ambitious Thoughts, in aspiring after Rule and Government. I'll warrant you, Sir, this will hide the Fact, and you shall never be discovered.

Presently upon this Motion, *Conscience* steps in, and spake after this Manner:

Consc. Sir, Do not this evil Deed, he is your only Brother; and his Blood will cry for Vengeance.

Sin. What dost do, my *Cain*? Why dost thou make a Pause?

Cain. I am hindered by a timorous Fellow in my House, whom I know not: Somebody I think hath sent him hither on purpose to be a Plague to me.

Sin. Regard him not; I will undertake to stifle him, and spoil his telling Tales. Go call thy Brother forth, and walk together in the Fields. Be sure carry it lovingly to him, lest he mistrust thee: I warrant you he will talk with you about Religion, and condemn your Way of Worship; and tho' he be

your

your younger Brother, yet he will undertake to teach thee; and if thou wilt be a Fool, and suffer it, do.

Cain. I will try that, so far I am resolved to take thy Counsel.

And immediately away he went and called his Brother forth; and they walked together in the Field.

Cain. Brother, what a vast Fabrick is here? This World in which we are placed, is full of great Wonders and excellent Rarities, and all after our Father *Adam* is dead, will be ours; all the Riches, I mean, and the Glory thereof: My Heart, Brother, is wonderfully pleased with the Thoughts of it; I desire no greater Glory nor Happiness, tho' I have heard my Father talk of a *future State* beyond the Grave that exceeds all Things here below.

Abel. Brother, this World, and all the Wonders we behold, doth shew forth the Glory and Handyworks of *Jehovah*, our Blessed God and Creator, whose we are, and whom we serve; for He is a jealous God, and executes Justice on the Earth; and is a Rewarder of all those who diligently seek Him.

Cain. You are a Fool: I do not believe there is any *Reward* for *Justice* and *Righteousness*, nor *Vengeance* for *Ungodliness*.

Abel. Brother, it grieves me to hear you speak after this Manner; for I have had Evidence of his Mercy, and favourable Acceptance already. I am afraid, truly, you are misled by some Enemy: The Way you go, Brother, is not good: Think upon the *World to come*.

Cain. Wisdom is only with you: I see how you are swoln up with Pride: Leave off your talking of a *World to come*, for I believe none.

B 6 *Abel.*

Abel. You shew a very wicked, naughty, and unbelieving Heart; I am ashamed to hear your Discourse.

Some Things of this Nature, we may suppose they might discourse of: And *Cain* being afresh moved to Wrath thereby, took the Devil's Counsel, and rose up and murdered him.

See the Rev. Mr. *Ainsworth* upon this Matter.*

*Cain *spake unto Abel his Brother; but what they said, is not set down. The Hebrew Text hath here a Pause extraordinary; implying* (saith he) *further Matter. The Greek Version addeth, Let us go out into the Field. And Thargum Jerusalemy addeth the same, and much more, viz. How Cain, when to y'* nowne *in the Field, should say, There was no Judgment, nor Judge, nor other World to come, nor Reward of Justice, nor Vengeance for Wickedness, &c. All which Abel gainsaid, and then his Brother slew him doth seemeth* (saith he) *to imply a Dissimulation of Cain's Hatred, in that friendly Converse with his Brother, till he found Opportunity to kill him.* See *Ainsw. Annotat. on Gen. 4. 5, 6, 7, Pag. 22.*

Thus this Enemy prevailed; and, in a second Attempt, overcame the Fourth Part of the World. But see how Sin and the *Devil* deceived *Cain.* The Murder was soon discovered; for lo, on a sudden, a mighty Cry was heard, *Vengeance! Vengeance! God,* who as the Searcher out of Blood, cries, *Where is Abel thy Brother?* Nothing can be hid from his Eye. Murder shall not go unpunished: *The Voice of thy Brother's Blood cries to me from the Ground.* Guilt follows his Sin with the dreadful Wrath of God: *And now thou art cursed from the Face of the Earth.* Behold the venomous Nature of this Tyrant! Seven Abominations he let into *Cain's* Heart at once: 1. To

The Travels of Ungodliness. 37

sacrifice without *Faith*. 2. And yet to be displeased that God respected him not. 3. Not to hearken to God's Admonition. 4. To speak dissemblingly when Mischief was in his Heart. 5. To kill his own and only *Brother*, and that for *Righteousness* Sake; and thereby to destroy, as much as in him lay, all the *Righteous Ones* that might have proceeded from his Loins. 6. To deny the *Fact*, by saying, *He knew not where he was*. 7. And, after all, asketh not for *Mercy*; but rather despaireth under the Sense of the *Punishment*, than convinced of the heinous Nature of his *Sin*: And so fell under the *Condemnation* of the Devil.

But to still, or rather stifle his *Conscience*; (if there was any left in him) *Sin*, and the *Devil* enticed him away from the Presence of God, or (as *Ainsworth* hath it) from God's Word, and Publick Worship, to dwell in the Land of *Nod*; and to divert his Thoughts, marry'd a Wife, and built a City, which might also be for his better Security from his Fears, &c.

After this, *Sin* proceeds further in his *Progress*; and, as he subdued all *Cain's* Seed in general, so more especially, he overcame *Lamech*. First, By violating the *Law of Marriage*. Secondly, In committing of *Murder*; and, Thirdly, In glorying in it: *I have killed a Man*, &c. *If he that killeth* Cain, *shall be punished seven-fold; then he that killeth Me, seventy-seven fold*.

It seemeth (faith an eminent Writer) *to be an insolent Contempt of God's Judgment, and abusing of his Patience towards* Cain, &c.

Time would fail me, to shew distinctly, how *Sin*, by his Subtilty, generally prevailed in those

Days,

Days, by alluring the Hearts of Men and Women with *Musical Instruments*, and other *Pleasures* and *sensual Delights* and *Profits* of this *World*. Yet God, to preserve a *Godly Seed*, that he might have a *Church* in all *Ages*, and fulfil his *Promise* to *Adam*, gave *Eve* another Son instead of *Abel*, whom *Cain* slew, whom she called *Seth*: Who was born (saith *Ainsworth*) not till One Hundred and Thirty Years after the Creation.

This *Seth* begat *Enos*, so he is called in *Greek*; in *Hebrew*, *Enosh*; that is, by Interpretation, *Sorrowful, Sick, Miserable*; so named, 'tis thought, from the Consideration of the woeful State of those Days. For it seems that *Sin* prevailed wonderfully (as worthy *Annotationers* make appear) by prophane calling on the Almighty, and by calling Idols by the Name of the Lord, and by making Images and Representations of Him. So high had *Apollyon* raised his Throne in those Times, that scarce One in a Thousand ('tis thought) but were subdued under his Feet, and became meer Vassals and Slaves to him. Yet *Godliness* soon after had one most choice and renowned Champion, who bravely overcame this Hellish Enemy, and walked with God Three Hundred Years. But the Lord seeing how *Ungodliness* every where abounded, took this Holy Person from these Lower Regions, to dwell with Him Above. But *Sin*, as on Eagle's Wings, pursued his Progress, and like a devouring and unsatisfy'd Monster, resolved to destroy the whole World again at once, or provoke the dreadful God of Heaven to do it; which in a short Space after he almost effected, by corrupting the Earth; that is, the Inhabitants of the Earth; nay, and the Earth

itself

itself (saith *Ainsworth*) by the abominable Pollution of that Generation was defiled; which agrees with another Text, *Isa.* xxiv. (*Sin* is of an infectious and poisonous Nature, fitly compared to the Plague of the Leprosy;) The Earth was defiled under the Inhabitants thereof. And this Corruption is especially applied to Idolatry, and depraving of God's True Worship, as appears by other Scriptures, *Exod.* iii. 7. *Deut.* xxxii. 5. *Judges* ii. 19. which was the grand Design *Apollyon* laboured to effect by this Hell-bred Agent. Nay, and the Disease was Epidemical: All Flesh was defiled, and their Way corrupted; that is, their *Faith* and *Religion*, and their *Manners, Works*, and *Course of Life*, &c. *Every Imagination and Thought of their Hearts were only evil, and that continually*: All were in love with, received and harboured this cursed Enemy: Every Door was open, and all Hearts prepared to embrace him, and bid him welcome; every Faculty of their Souls being depraved and overcome by him, so that none but *Sin* and the Devil was regarded and subjected to by them of that Generation. *God* and *Godliness* were had in great Contempt. The whole World seemed to be but a Mass of Filth and detestable Corruption. The Sons of God, that is, Men of the *Church*, or Children of *Seth*, were by the Power of this Enemy, brought to mix or mingle themselves by unlawful Marriages, &c. with the Daughters of Men, *viz.* the Offspring of *Cain*, the *Cursed Seed*. Nothing but Violence, Oppression, Injurious and Cruel Dealing overspread the whole World. No Fear of God, nor Regard of Men; Rapine, Spoil and Murder aboundeth in all Places;

and

and yet they seemed to live free from Fear, and in the greatest Security imaginable, Buying and Selling, Building and Planting, Marrying, and being given in Marriage.

But now see what followeth: The Vengeance of God pursues the Traveller; Heaven could not bear longer with such prodigious Wickedness: And therefore that God might shew his Wrath upon those who had cast him off, from whom they had their Breath and Being, behold what a mighty Flood of Water approaches! Now nothing but Death! Their Joy is turned into Sorrow, and their Mirth into Mourning. Now the Heavens weep, and their Eyes pour forth Showers too; but their Cries and Tears will not atone for their Sins, for the Flood came, and took them all away.

Adieu, false World: See, see thy fearful Fate!
Alas, thou would'st not see it, till too late!
What hast thou got (come speak) by letting in
And entertaining of this Monster Sin?
See, how thy Enemy, and Hellish Foe
Doth laugh at this thy fatal Overthrow:
Vengeance pursues, and will o'ertake all those
Who God despise, and with the Devil close.

But all were not destroyed; for *Noah* before this Time had entertained *True Godliness*, and thereby was delivered from the Flood. *Thee* (saith the Lord) *only have I found righteous before Me, in this Generation: Come thou, and thy House, into the Ark.* And by this Means was *Ham* spared, who was of the *Seed* of the *Serpent*.

And hereby *Apollyon* had the better Opportunity to save the *cursed Traveller*, who brought that fearful

ful Overthrow upon the *Old World*, the Effect of God; but the Cause was not utterly removed: The Sinner was drowned, but not *Sin*; but contrarywise, he got fresh Strength and Power, and pursued his Progress with as great Rage as ever; and, like another great and overflowing Deluge, threatned Spiritually to drown and destroy the World again in such Sort, as if That Flood was but a Type or Figure of This.

Two Floods I read of; One was caus'd by Sin,
That was Eternal; the Other flows within.
Noah escap'd the First, such Favour found;
But afterwards, by This, was almost drown'd.
The former Flood of Water did extend
But some few Days: When will the Other end?
They both destroy'd: But Sin is far the worst:
And 'tis more general too than was the First.
Waters shall drown no more, a Sign God hath giv'n:
When shall we see a Rainbow after Sin?

After this, as the World multiplied and encreased in Number, so did *Sin* grow in Strength and Policy, and the *Children of Men* went to build great *Babel*, which was a crafty Device of *Apollyon*; but God defeated that Counsel, and confounded their *Language*; and then they were forced into all the Quarters of the Earth. But this *Traveller* pursued them all, where-ever they went, and made them all subject to his Authority, and become Servants to *Lucifer*, &c. for he drew them to *Idolatry*, and defiled them with all manner of gross *Pollution* and *Sensuality*; insomuch that Four great Cities, viz. *Sodom, Gomorrah, Adamah,* and *Zeboam,* were totally laid waste by him, and became an eternal Monument

...ent of God's fearful Wrath. For as this Enemy filled their Hearts, and set them on Fire with *Unnatural Lusts*, as *Whoredom, Incest*, and *Sodomy*; the Men leaving the natural Use of the Woman, burned in Lust one towards another, even Men with Men, working that which is unseemly and abominable) so God destroyed them with Fire and Brimstone; which made them at last, when it was too late, cry out,

> Curs'd be the Day that we let in
>   This cruel Enemy:
> O! it is He, this Monster SIN,
>   That makes us thus to fry!
> These Flames are sad, which on us cease:
>   But we, too late, do cry;
> For we shall bear worse Pains than these,
>   To all Eternity.

Yet God raised up a few in every Age, to witness against *Sin*, and undermine his Kingdom, as *Abraham* and *Lot*; but *Lot* in one Encounter was worsted, (tho' a brave Champion in his Days for *True Godliness*;) afterwards *Isaac*, and then *Jacob*, who was a Prince with God. But that which proved effectual for the weakening of *Sin*'s Power, was the *Covenant* concerning the *Woman's Seed*; which was afresh renewed to these *Patriarchs*. After this God raised up *Joseph* and his *Brethren*. This *Joseph* proved a mighty Man of Valour: For notwithstanding the Power and Policy of *Apollyon*, and all the whole Infernal Lake, this Heavenly Warrior could not be made to yield: He neither regarded Frowns nor Flatteries; and the main Ground of his constant Resistance was, because he saw what a hateful Enemy *Sin* was in God's Sight.

How

44 *The* Progress *of* SIN: Or,

How shall I do this Thing and sin against God? That was the Weapon by which he overcame; yet nevertheless, his *Brethren*, tho' they took up Arms against *Sin*, were sorely worsted by him, and particularly, being moved with Envy, *Sold poor Joseph into* Egypt, *but God was with him*, and he came off at last, a *glorious Conqueror*, (though the Enemy by Policy, once put him to Flight: When he lived in Pomp and Glory in *Pharaoh's* Court, he learned to swear, *By the Life of* Pharaoh;) but by Means of *Conscience*, a noble Officer for the *Prince of Light*, *Joseph's Brethren* did recover from the Fall *Sin* gave them, for he made them cry out, *We were verily guilty concerning our Brother*, &c. From these Mens Loins afterwards a great Army arose or sprung up, who did wonderful Exploits against this malicious Traveller and Champion of Hell; they having at first, upon the Death of *Joseph* and his Brethren, a brave and victorious Captain to command them, called *Moses*; yet these possessed but a small Spot of Ground in comparison of the whole Universe: And as touching the greatest Part of the World, *Sin* wholly ruled and tyrannized over them, and they became meer Slaves and Drudges to the Devil; so that of them we shall take but little more Notice, but speak somewhat of *Moses*, that Man of God, the Prince and chief Leader of *Israel*.

This Man at first was under dangerous Circumstances, being brought up amongst the Friends and Servants of *Apollyon*; who to entice him to his Party, offered him all the Pleasures and Honours of *Pharaoh's* Court; and 'tis thought if he had deserted his Prince, and took up Arms for the Enemy,

he

might after *Pharaoh*'s Death have been crowned King of *Egypt*: But he having a mighty Shield in his Hand, and being also otherwise compleatly armed, put the Enemy to Flight, and *chose rather to suffer Affliction with the People of God, than to enjoy the Pleasures that this cunning Deceiver offered him for a Season*. But upon this, a sore and grievous War fell out between the two *Seeds*; for *Pharaoh* by no Means would tolerate or give Liberty to *True Godliness* to live amongst them. But, for this their Wrath and Enmity, he, with the *Egyptians*, paid dear; for *Sin*, with implacable Malice, so hardened his Heart, that notwithstanding Ten terrible Plagues, he would not suffer the Children of *Israel* to *go and worship the Lord their God*: Therefore *Jehovah* at last destroyed them all in the *Red Sea*.

Now after the Overthrow of the *Egyptians*, *Sin* stirred up all his Powers to corrupt the *Holy Seed*, and prevailed also exceedingly; insomuch that many of *them turned Idolaters, and forsook the True God*. Now, some Time before this, *Jehovah*, to convince them of the miserable Condition they were in, by entertaining this Enemy, he gave forth a holy and severe *Law* in a *Burning* and *Fiery Mountain*; and by reason of the Depravity of their Hearts, and Weakness of their Hands through the Flesh, that *Law* greatly strengthened *Sin*, and laid them and the whole World under Guilt, and the heavy Wrath of an angry God; and many were cut off by the Hand of Justice. (For Temporal Death, as was Eternal, was denounced as the Punishment of every Transgression and Disobedience thereof.) Yet God, that *Sin* might not thereby triumph

triumph and vaunt himself above Measure, graciously added another *Law*; that by the *Types*, *Shadows*, and *Sacrifices* of it, they might by the Help of *Faith*, see a Remedy; which was by the Death of the *Messiah*, who was promised long before.

And now from that Time until the Coming of Christ, 'tis needless for me to speak further of *The Progress of* Sin; or, *The Travels of* Ungodliness: The fearful Exploits he did to the Seven Nations of the Land of *Canaan*, whom he utterly destroyed, and gave up to God's Sin's-revenging Hand; and also how by his Subtilty he overcame the Children of *Israel* in the *Wilderness*, and when they came into the *Land of Promise*, of which you may read at large in the Sacred History; and Time would fail me to run through.

Moreover, he laid all Kingdoms of the Earth weltering in their Blood, and made them groan under his heavy Yoke and Tyranny. In a Word, many Millions of Souls fell by his Hands, and divers grievous Plagues and Judgments for his Sake were inflicted upon poor Mortals, almost every where. Some who were his Enemies, and Lovers of *Godliness*, he stirred up his Emissaries to *starve to Death*, to *burn alive*, *saw asunder*, and *throw into Lyons Dens to be torn to Pieces*, and others to be *stoned*: So that all that opposed him, or would not give him Entertainment, were forced to *wander about in Sheeps-skins and Goats-skins, being destitute, afflicted and tormented*. And what was most lamentable, was, to find many Thousands of them who professed themselves to be God's People, (nay, and Leaders amongst them) so grievously deceived by him, that they became his meer Vassals, and acted

much

...ch of the sad Tragedy upon the *Holy Seed*; in...uch, that *Ahab*, who was a Prince in *Israel*, ...l himself to work Wickedness.

Neither did they who were his professed Friends ...Servants, speed much better in this World; ...he caused many of his Admirers to sacrifice ...r poor Children to *Moloch*, which was to throw ...m into *a fierce Fire, and burn them to Death*: *y burnt their Sons and Daughters*, saith Sacred ...xt, *and sacrificed them unto Devils, and shed in*...*nt Blood*, &c. and others he stirred up with ...ath and Malice to fight against, and destroy ...another; so that every Part of God's Law ...ght be violated and trodden under his Feet: ...d *Jehovah*, to revenge himself upon them for ...e Love and Kindness they shewed to this *Murderer*, brought the *Sword*, *Famine*, and *Pestilence*, and other amazing Judgments upon them; so that by this Tyrant's Means were many made Fatherless, and others Widows; nay, no Misery that Man's Heart can imagine, or mortal Creatures be capable to suffer, but he with Vengeance brought it upon *Adam*'s Seed, throughout the whole Universe. Nay, and he so blinded their Eyes, that, in some Nations, he caused many People to worship the Sun, Moon, and Stars, and at last, the Devil himself, whom they called an evil God, because he tormented them; and they durst do no less than adore him, for fear he otherwise would destroy them.

Thus did this Enemy tyrannize after a most lamentable Manner; neither was there any able (finally) to overcome him, but the Man *Christ*; by which Means he did even almost what he pleased,

destroying

destroying Body and Soul too, and none could get out of his Hand, but they who looked upon *Jesus* who was promised, and long-looked and waited for. Now, these Things considered, the Coming of the *Messiah* must needs be acknowledged, an inconceivable Blessing to Mankind, who were thus spoiled, torn in Pieces, and fearfully tormented by this cruel Enemy. And indeed, great was the Expectation and Breathings that were amongst those who were sensible of that dismal State the World and their own Souls were in.

But hold! I must stop again; for I hear the *Saviour* and *Glorious Messiah*, and *Prince of Righteousness* is come! Blessed News, indeed! Sing, O Heaven; and rejoice, O Earth! *Glory to God in the Highest, and on Earth, Good-will to Men!*

But what Provision is made to entertain Him? Do they not look out some stately Palace for Him? And do not Thousands and Ten Thousands swarm about Him, to congratulate his Arrival, with all Expressions of Joy imaginable? For, O the Worth of his *Person*, the Greatness of his *Glory*, and the Nature of that *Work* He is come to do! Never before appeared such a *Saviour* and *Deliverer!* Now the *Destroyer* of *Tyrant Sin*, with the *Devil*, and all the *Powers* of *Hell* is come! He is come! Aye, but where doth He Lodge the first Night? Is the *best Chamber* shewed Him, and a *Down-Bed* ready made and prepared for Him?

No, no; *Sin* has got the chief Room in the *Inn*, I mean, the *Heart*; and the *Heavenly Prince* is forced to go into the *Stable*, and take up his Lodging in the *Manger*. Oh! do not they deserve to be deceived and ruined for ever, who hug, delight

delight in, and kindly entertain their Enemy, he that seeks to destroy them; (who whilst he smiles i their Faces, secretly designs to cut their Throats) nd slight after this Sort, their only Friend, nay, ieir right and lawful *Prince* and *Sovereign*; whom l their Fathers, Holy Men, and Blessed Prohets prophesied of, rejoicing to think of this Day? And shall He be turned into the *Stable*? What le, who hath Millions of Holy Angels to attend him; whom the Glorious *Seraphims* and *Cherubims* do adore and fall down before. Is this the Welcome and Entertainment which poor Mankind do allot Him, who was the Joy and Delight of his Heart, and for whose Sake He is come to revenge Himself, and utterly overcome *Sin*, and so destroy the Works of the Devil?

Moreover, after this, the glorious *Prince* was most basely and evilly entreated by *Apollyon* and his Emissaries; for this crafty Enemy blinded the Eyes of the poor *Jews*, in such Sort, that they would not know him, nor believe he was the *Messiah* and Mighty *Saviour* promised to their Fathers; and hereby *Sin* got such hold of them, as to stir them up to load him with all manner of Infamy; calling him, *a Wine-bibber, a gluttonous Person, &c. a Friend to Publicans and Sinners*: Nay, caused some of them to cry out, *He had a Devil, and is mad;* and that *He cast out Devils by* Belzebub *the Prince of Devils*: And all this they did, and much more, to make him odious in the Eyes of the People, that so none might fly to him for Help and Salvation from this bloody and devouring Enemy. And at last, the whole *Infernal Lake* consulted together, to stir up the *High-Priest* and *chief Rulers*; (having

filled

filled their Hearts with Envy and cursed Hatred, to accuse him with *Blasphemy*, *Sedition*, and *Treason*, that so He might as a notorious *Criminal* or *Malefactor* be put to Death; which Thing indeed He came on purpose to do, viz. to Die, tho' it was hid from them: For had *Apollyon* known that the Death of Christ was the only Way to destroy the Power of *Sin*, *Death*, and the *Grave*, and utterly spoil and bring down his own Kingdom, he doubtless would never have promoted that Work.

But so it was, the Creature Man being by the Power and Subtilty of *Sin*, brought under the Breach of God's Holy Law, which denounceth *Death* upon every *Transgressor* thereof; by which Means *the whole World became guilty before God* of the highest Treason, &c. owing more than Ten Thousand Talents to Divine Justice, and had nothing to pay: Now, the Lord Jesus, out of *Infinite Love*, offered himself as the Creature's Surety, to undertake, and answer all the just Demands of the Law, and make a compleat Compensation to Justice for all the Wrong Man had done, by yielding to this Hellish Tyrant, to the manifest Violation of the Law, &c. And since without shedding of Blood, there could be no Remission of the horrible Crimes he stood charged with, he laid down his Life; that so by *Death* he might make an End of *Sin*, as to his condemning Quality, and *destroy Him who had the Power of* Death, *which is the* Devil; *and deliver Them, who through the Fear of* Death *were all their Life-time subject to Bondage*, Heb. ii.

That Work must needs be carried on indeed,
When Heav'n and Hell about it are agreed:

Tho' different Ends in those great Agents are,
Yet in the Thing they both agreed were:
That Christ should be of his dear Life depriv'd,
Tho' Hell alone the guilty Act contriv'd.
Yet God indeed, from all Eternity,
Knowing what Rage and curs'd Malignity
Would be in their base Hearts, resolved then
He would permit and suffer those vile Men
To bring his Purpose and Decree to pass,
Which for our Good and his own Glory was.

How wonderfully was the grand Enemy by this mischievous Design baffled and overcome! For that very Way that *Sin* and the Devil thought utterly to destroy the Hopes and Help of poor Mortals, God took to save them; for lo, after Three Days, the Glorious Prince arose from the Dead, to the great Terror and Consternation of all the Powers of Darkness. But after this, *Sin* mightily prevailed, and but a very few Persons obtained Deliverance; for he caused the *Jews* to require a *Sign*, and the Learned *Greeks* to seek after *Wisdom* (for *Natural* and *Moral Philosophy* about that Time, seemed to be the great Idol of the World, it being in the Top of its Glory:) And by these Means the *Gospel* became a Stumbling-block to the one, and Foolishness to the other; and such who did receive the *Truth*, by the Rage and Subtilty of *Apollyon*, were exposed to sore and grievous Persecutions: For now nothing but Blood and Slaughter the Enemy raised upon all those who listed themselves under Christ's Banner; so that in the Space of Three Hundred Years, Millions of Christians were tortured and barbarously murdered; and all by the Means and Instigation of this cruel Enemy.

52 *The* Progress *of* SIN: Or,

Nay, and should we proceed to shew, before and after these Times, the many Ways and cunning Stratagems the Wicked devised, to continue, enlarge, and establish *Apollyon*'s Hellish Kingdom, it would fill great Volumes.

1. They endeavoured to blacken the Followers of *Godliness* with all manner of horrid Crimes imaginable, to the End that all ignorant People might not be won, or brought over to close with them; but contrariwise loath and hate them, and be moved without Remorse or Pity, to reproach, persecute, and inflict all manner of Cruelties upon their poor frail and innocent Bodies; for they put the *Christians*, as some observe, into *Bears-skins*, and then set on the Dogs to worry them.

2. He caused many who seemed Lovers of the *Gospel*, and Professors of it, to cast it off, and embrace the Vanities of the World; nay, to worship *Idols*, and to sacrifice to them.

3. He raised up Multitudes to foment most abominable Errors and Heresies in the Church; by which Means the Truth suffered greatly, and the Devil got much Ground, and strengthened his Kingdom; which is signified in part, by that great Flood the *Dragon* cast out of his Mouth to drown the *Woman* and her *Seed* who kept the Commandments of God, and had the Testimony of Jesus Christ. But this was not all; for *Apollyon* had a greater Design in this Age of the World on foot, which was two-fold: One was to introduce *Mahomet*, and compile the *Turkish Alcoran*, by which Means Millions of Millions have been deceived to this Day; a strange Hodgpodge, ridiculous and Flesh-pleasing Religion, (if it may be called Religion.)

gion.) This began about the Year Six Hundred.

2. To usher in and set up a more Visible, Spiritual, or Ecclesiastical State on Earth, than ever he had before since the Beginning of the World, attended with external Glory and outward Grandeur, which in the Apostles Days he had laid the Foundation of; but till the *Sixth Head*, or *Imperial Power* was removed, he could not thoroughly effect nor establish, (which fell out between Four and Five Hundred Years after Christ.) And to the End he might accomplish it, *Apollyon* saw it would be necessary to get the Hellish Enemy to do the Work for him, who in the Scripture is called, *The Man of Sin*. And tho' I represent him here as a *Servant*, yet the Devil resolved to make him a *Lord*; yea, a *Lord of Lords*; nay, no less than a *God*; and to exalt him far above all that are called *Gods*; yea, above the *God of Gods*; and to set him in the *Temple*, viz. the *Church*, to shew himself to be *God*, that is, to assume that to himself, which only belongs to the ever *Blessed God*. This is he who hath been brought in after the *Working of Satan, with all Power, Signs, and Lying Wonders; and with all Deceiveableness of Unrighteousness in them that perish*, &c. This is he whom they call *Head and Husband of the Church*; the *Vicar of Christ* over the whole World; *God's Vicegerent*; *Peter's Successor*; the *Head and Center of Unity*: But, in the Scripture, called *Anti-Christ*; the *Man of Sin*; the *Son of Perdition*; the *Beast that came out of the Earth with two Horns like a Lamb, but a Voice like a Dragon*; the *False Prophet*; the *Idle Shepherd*, and *Evil Servant*: And indeed, the only *Universal Head* of this *False Church*, or *Ecclesiastical State*,

that

54　*The* Progress *of* SIN: *Or,*

that *Apollyon* hath introduced or set up, by the Help of *Sin*, in the World, to deceive, ruin, and destroy the Souls of Men.

Sin now began to brandish his victorious Sword, and vaunt himself in his *Diabolical Sovereignty*. If you are for *Religion*, or will be *Religious*, you shall have one that shall suit your *sensual Appetites*, and will agree with your *worldly Interest*. For when *Apollyon* saw that the inward *Life* and *Power* of the *Christian Religion* was generally gone, and yet the People affected the Name of *Christ*, and would not be satisfy'd without some Way or Manner of *Worship*, then he began to erect this false Form and Image of *Christianity*, or set up *Counterfeit Godliness*: And since Men knew not what belonged to the inward Beauty and Glory of *Grace* and *True Godliness*, he was resolved to make it up in an outward Manner, that it might appear amiable to all such that had no more than Fleshly Eyes to see with.

The Enemy at this Time roared like a mighty and over-grown Monster, and sent out *Bulls*, threatning to destroy and devour all who would not worship the *Beast* and his *Image*, or receive his *Mark* in their *Foreheads*: Nay, in good Earnest, those who would not sacrifice their *Reason*, *Conscience*, and *Religion* to the *Lust* and *Ambition* of this Tyrant, and adore his *Golden Image*, were not to be suffered to Buy nor Sell, nor indeed to Live; and therefore he devised, by the Help of *Apollyon*, all Sorts of cruel Tortures and Torments to be inflicted on all Manner of People, both Young and Old, High and Low, Rich and Poor, Bond and Free, who refused to worship Gods of *Gold*, *Silver*, *Brass*, *Iron*; nay, and a strange Idol he had made

The Travels of Ungodliness.

of a *Wafer-Cake*; by which Means they murdered many Thousands, if not Millions of Thousands, of the poor, innocent Saints and Servants of God, in such Sort, that every Street of the great City *Babylon*, became like a meer Shambles to quarter out the Limbs of Men, Women, and Children; Ten, Twenty, Thirty, Forty, an Hundred, nay, Two Hundred Thousand Souls have been sacrificed before they did give over; as witness the *Irish Massacre*, &c. Some he caused to be *Burned*, some to be *Roasted alive*, some their *Skins flea'd off*, others *Hanged by the Hairs of their Heads*; *Poisoning, Starving, Drowning*, and any other Kind of Death *Apollyon* could devise, were the poor Saints and Lovers of *True Godliness* put to, and that by such who called themselves *Christians*.

But, since we have brought him down very near to the Days wherein we Live, and also hear he is still upon his *Progress*, wandering up and down in as eager Pursuit of his Hellish Enterprize as ever; Let us now give over, and treat of his *present Travels* in this, and other Nations.

CHAP. IV.

Shewing how Peccatum, *alias* Sin, *came into a Country called* Non-Age; *and of the strange Projects he played there.*

WE having brought down our History of this cruel Enemy to these latter Times, 'tis very necessary to give you some Account of his *present Travels*, and shew what *Progress* he makes

The Progress of SIN: Or,

among the People of this Generation: And that we may do it the better, we shall begin with his entering into a great, tho' weak Country, called *Non-Age*; (he having Intelligence from *Apollyon*, that a great Number of feeble People, of a small Stature, were two or three Years ago, by common Fate, tho' through much Difficulty, come into this Kingdom, and for a short Time were to continue in this Country, he was resolved to visit them.) But the *Prince of Darkness* understanding that this Enterprize was of great Importance, and might tend very much, if well managed, to the *Increasing, Strengthening,* and *Enlarging* of his Kingdom, or otherwise, prove to the great Hurt thereof; first called a Council in Hell, to advise what was fittest to be done at this Juncture. And having held their treacherous Consultations, and come to Agreement, *Apollyon* with winged Speed, repairs to *Peccatum,* alias *Sin,* to suggest to him what was agreed upon, and to instruct him how to manage his Affairs in the Country of *Non-Age*; whom he addressed himself to after this Manner:

Most Dear and Mighty Peccatum, *the Great Lord and Conqueror of the World, the Envy of Heaven, and chief Darling of Hell: Seeing thou hast been always true to our Interest, and hast raised up our Kingdom above all Kingdoms of the Earth, and made my Glory, Fame, and Grandeur to spread abroad far and near; I have some few Instructions to impart to thee, of great Importance, upon thy entering into this Country, to the End thou mayest make ready a great People for my Service, and to fight under my Banner: For those which I now send thee to, thou must train up from the Cradle, (as my Great Servant and Beloved Emperor*

Emperor Mahomet *doth his* Janizaries) *that they may be well instructed in our Politicks, and skilful in all Stratagems of War against* God, Christ, *and True Godliness, with all his Retinue. This is the Time for thee to work, and the best Age of Mankind to work upon: 'Tis good to sow our Seed timely, and to take Possession before we are supplanted by our Enemy; for 'tis easier to prevent a Disease, than to cure it; or to keep an Adversary out, than when he is in, to get rid of him. And one Thing, to my Joy, I will tell thee between thee and I: A long Time ago, before any of this Army entered into these Parts, thou, in a great Measure, didst their Business for them; for as they come into these Regions, they bring with them Trophies of thy Conquest over them: For thou didst indeed, originally, season and leaven their Natures for me in such sort, that they all declare, as one Man, whose Side they resolve to take, and under whose Banner they are inclined to Fight. Yet nevertheless, there is much Work for us to do, lest in their tender Age, by Means of what they call* Godly Education, *their Hearts secretly should be drawn away from us, by seasoning them with Grace, or such Principles that will prove very destructive to our Interest. Therefore, to prevent all the Danger that may arise, thou must chuse Tutors for all this young and hopeful Progeny, or have a great Hand in the Education of them; which if we can work about, we shall do our Business effectually: But considering the divers* Ranks, Degrees, Qualities, Descent, *or Pedigree of them, thou must find out suitable Tutors accordingly, but all of thine own Offspring.*

Now, no sooner had *Sin* received his Instructions, but he hasted away as on Eagle's Wings, and suddenly invaded the whole Country of *New-Age*.

58　*The Progress of* SIN: Or,

And to the End he might fully effect this Hellish Intrigue, he resolved that a great Part of the *Weak* and *Feeble Inhabitants* should be Tutor'd by Mrs. *Ignorance*; to whom *Apollyon* directed his Speech after this Sort:

Apol. *My dear Cousin and Friend; I have a great Number of pretty Boys and Girls for you to Tutor and bring up for me in the Country of* Non-Age: *Will you undertake the Charge?*

Ignor. *Most Dread and Mighty* Apollyon! *You know I never yet declined any Drudgery for you, which lay in my Power. My Lord, I am ready to obey you.*

Apol. *I assure you, Madam, I kindly accept of all your former and latter Services, and cannot but acknowledge you have done strange Things for the Advancement of my Kingdom, and greatning my Power in the World.*

And now, Noble Peccatum, *this Gentlewoman, Madam* Ignorance, *is your Child; your natural Offspring, your own Flesh and Blood; nay, a Limb or Member of your Body: Therefore I charge you to help and assist her in this great Work; for I should be glad if she had the Education of all the Children in the whole World, I have such a Veneration for her.*

Sin, upon this, immediately laid about him, and indeed wonderfully succeeded in this his first Attempt, by the Help of the *Prince of Darkness*; insomuch that Abundance of those poor Souls, whereof none were above the Age of Twelve or Fourteen Years, were trained up in gross *Ignorance* and *Blindness of Mind,* understanding little or nothing of God, Christ, or the Gospel; no, nor of their own woeful State and Condition (the Enemy both formerly and latterly had brought them into) and this he effected many Ways.

First,

First, By keeping their Parents, and such who were to instruct them, under the Power of *sottish Ignorance*; so that they who should be as *Eyes* to the *Blind*, and *Feet* to the *Lame*, had no *Eyes* to see, nor *Feet* to go themselves.

2. He represented to many Parents, the great Charge of putting their Offspring to School; persuading them (they being poor and low in the World) they could not be at the Cost, tho' they bestowed a great deal more needlesly upon cloathing and feeding of them, than their Learning would have came to.

Now, the Reason why the Enemy is so greatly set against *Learning*; is this: Lest by their attaining to the Knowledge of Letters, they should take to Read the *Holy Bible*, which he dreads exceedingly; because when understood, it vanquisheth (at once) his *Darling Ignorance*.

3. He endeavours to prevent their learning any *pious Catechism* that is founded upon the Authority of the *Holy Scripture*.

4. By hindering them, as much as possible, from discoursing or asking Questions about *God*, *Christ*, and *Religion*. Also by causing Parents to be careless about, or rather against, their going to *Church*, where the *Word* of *God* is truly and powerfully Preached, and the *Sacraments* duly and truly Administred.

5. By taking off the Childrens Hearts from any Thing that concerns their *Souls*; or a *Future State*; by filling their Heads with Vanities, Toys, and Trifles of a Childhood State.

6. By presenting to Parents (who understand more than they intend to practise) the *Knowledge* of

God

God a dangerous Thing; and that they who are most *spiritually wise*, were like to be most *miserable* in the World.

7. By persuading some, that the *Matters* of *God* and *Religion* only belonged to *Ministers*; and that others should only mind their *Trades*; as if the *Trade* or *Calling* of *Godliness* did not belong to all *Parents* and *Children* to learn; it being the main Business that all Mortals were sent into this World to follow.

8. By presenting the Example of all generally, within Doors and without, Abroad and at Home before their Eyes; and there being little or nothing (as the poor *Children* could see by any, either *Parents* or *Companions*) of a *Heavenly Nature*; but contrariwise, the *Evil Motions* and *Lusts* of this Enemy was wholly followed, who having subdued the *Strong*, (by the powerful Hand of his *Darling Ignorance*) might, and doth hereby easily invade and overcome the *Poor* and *Feeble*; and that, partly by the Means of that evil Example they have continually before their Eyes.

9. By tempting them (and others, much older than they) to conclude, that they shall have Time and Opportunity hereafter, and better Advantages to learn those great Things; which the Enemy tells them, are too high and sublime for their tender Age to pry into, understand, or make Judgment of. And thus the Devilish Enemy keeps some, nay, a great Part of the poor Inhabitants of the Country or Town of *Non-Age*, wholly ignorant of those Things which chiefly concerns them, and in their *Childhood-State* ought to look after; lest Satan by taking Possession so early in their

their Hearts, makes them afterwards, with much Ease, to become his meer Slaves and Vassals. And sad it is to see what Work *Sin* makes on *Little Ones*.

10. And lastly, *Sin* and the Devil keep them in *Ignorance*, by causing many of them to be trained up under a *blind* and *Soul-deceiving Ministry*.

But, alas! *Sin* hath not only this *Blind Tutor* to instruct the poor beguiled Progeny, but another as bad as She (and as you heard, of *Apollyon*'s own chusing too) *viz.* one *Pride*, to whom he also gave Instructions of a pernicious Nature, whereby some Thousands of them are wholly overcome, brought under the Power of this Deceiver, and undone for ever. This Varlet, it seems, is the Natural Off-spring of *Lucifer*, and doth not a little resemble him: And sad it is, that any *Little Ones* of Human Race should be brought up, and Tutor'd by her; she being one that the *Lord* greatly hateth, and will destroy at last all such who give themselves up to learn of her.

Now the Way that *Sin* takes to effect his Design by this Hellish Incendiary, is, *First*, To stir up *Little Ones*, according as he finds their Inclinations, before Ten Years are gone over their Heads, to delight in Fine Cloaths, and get into the Newest Fashion, tho' never so Foolish and Antick. And, *Secondly*, By sly Suggestions to allure their *Parents* to please their *Children*, and feed their natural (tho' unlawful and pernicious) Appetites herein: And that they may fully declare they are the real Slaves of *Lucifer*, and this his *Darling*, they betimes send their *Little Daughters* to School, to learn to *Dance*, as *Herodias* did. Here they learn to deck their *Fingers* with *Rings*, their *Ears* with *Jewels*, and their

their *Necks* with rich *Bracelets*, or *Necklaces* of *Gold* and *Pearl*; whereby they seem rather like little *Morris-Dancers*, than the young Offspring of *Christian People*. And thus, being bravely dressed up, and the Sparks of *Pride* kindled in them, they go with stretched-out *Necks*, and haughty *Hearts*, that in a short Time they are too high and proud to know almost any Body; and no Wonder, when they were never taught to know themselves.

And then, presently upon this, in comes Madam *Wanton*, to teach them other rare Inventions, viz. How to make *Set-Faces*, to cringe *A-la-mode de France*, the *sober Smile*, the *quaintest Dialect*; to humour *Discourse* well; to cast *Amorous Glances*, read *Love-Romances*, and frequent *Play-houses*; and also to provide Store of rare, tho' obscene *Draughts* or *Pictures*.

But to proceed: *Indulgence* and *Fond-Love*, as it appears, have their Charge and Instructions from the *Prince of Darkness*, to Tutor divers of them: And this the Enemy effects through great Subtilty, by infusing the *base Seed* into their *Hearts*; of which those two Varlets, *Indulgence* and *Fond-Love* were begot. Now those Parents in whom they bear Sway, are taught to indulge their Children in all Manner of Vices and evil Courses. Such dear and tender *Love* (or rather *Hatred*) they have towards their poor Offspring, that great Faults and filthy Enormities are winked at; and they must not be struck, nor hardly frowned on by any Means: Besides, should they whip, or severely chastise them, and they die soon after, how would it wound their Consciences? ('tis no Matter what becomes of their Souls) they are not troubled about

such

such Matters: Their great Care is to see they are well fed (tho' it be like Lambs for the Slaughter) and bravely cloath'd, and pamper'd up in those Ways they naturally love. And tho' they should Lie, Curse, Swear, or break the *Lord's Day*, and play when they should attend upon *God's Word*, or read the *Holy Bible*, it must with a gentle Reproof, or none at all, be passed by; remembring, when they were at their Age, they did the like themselves. The fond *Father* dares not tell the *Child's* Fault to his *Mother*; nor the fond *Mother* to the *Father*, lest he be angry; and to save his *Child's* Soul from Hell, sends his Head to the Wall, or rather with Discretion, wisely chastiseth him with a smarting Rod till the Blood comes. Alas! these seem to me to be the worst Tutors of all, because they lay in Fuel for every hurtful and devouring Fire, or prompt on and nourish every cursed Vice; and so open a Door for whole Legions of Devils to enter together, and make miserable Slaughter of their poor undone Progeny. These bring the *Parents* to Shame, the *Family* to Beggary, the *Child* to the Gallows, and his *Soul* to Hell.

Nay, these two Bloody Monsters, *Indulgence* and *Fond Love*, let in another destructive Tutor, who taught them to *Lie*, *Dissemble*, and *Equivocate*; so that in a short Time there was no believing hardly a Word the poor *Children* spoke. For having told two or three notorious Lies, and escaped with a little Chiding, without Correction, they grew very impudent and vile, not caring what they said to excuse themselves, when taken in other Faults. And not only *Hate-Truth*, but *Stubborn* and *Self-Will* also, by this very Means, came

came to be their Tutors also, to help *Apollyon* to make a perfect Conquest over them, and gave *Sin* full Possession: For hereby they became very rebellious, contradicting their Parents, making Mouths at them, not regarding what they commanded them to do, unless in a good Mood, but would pout and be sullen, or else crossly answer again, and strive to have the last Word.

And thus, by the Temptations of *Sin*, together with the natural Evil Disposition of their own Hearts, and Assistance of these cursed Tutors, *Apollyon* gave them Wings to fly whither-soever their unbounded, stubborn, and self-pleasing Wills led them, till they became fit Inhabitants for the City *Sensuality*.

But the Enemy seeing many of the Young Progeny in the Country of *Non-Age* were of a base, poor, and ignoble Race and Pedigree, their Parents not knowing well how to live themselves, without Pilfering and Stealing; one *Light-Fingers* was let in, who became Tutor to this Sort, and some others also, who were sent to her from *Pride*, *Wanton*, *Indulgence*, and *Fond-Love*; whom she taught the Art of *Thievery*. First, How to rob Orchards, to pull Quills out of the Wings of poor Geese, to milk Cows, &c. Afterwards, when they became good Proficients in their Alphabet, they learned harder Lessons; as, How to rob their Parents, Masters and Mistresses; and at last, the Art of Cheating, and Picking of Pockets, yea, and Locks too. And to the End they may perform this with the more Dexterity, they are quickly brought acquainted with the chief Masters of that Society, and learn the Cant Terms used by the

whole

The Travels of Ungodliness. 65

whole Corporation of *Thieves* and *Beggars*. Now these being little of Stature, are useful to the Company, because they can get in at Windows, and at other Places where the *older Thieves* cannot enter: And also, because of their tender Age, they are not suspected; or if taken, are like upon that Account to have more Pity shewed them; so that having great Encouragement, in a little Time they become perfect Masters of their Hellish Craft, and thereby are quite overcome by this bloody Enemy.

The last Tutor *Apollyon* chuses for the Young Progeny in the State or Country of *Non-Age*, is his Beloved (though Erroneous and Blasphemous) Daughter, *Misbelief*, alias *False-Faith*; and indeed there are not a few of them that are Educated by Her, by reason their Parents were utterly drawn aside from the True *Faith*, or Antient *Religion*, and led into the By-ways of *Schism*, *Heresy*, and *Error*, their poor Offspring are trained up in the same destructive and pernicious Ways; so that they hardly hold, or are established in one *Fundamental Principle* of the True *Religion*, by which Means they become *Papists*, *Atheists*, *Ranters*, *Arians*, *Socinians*, *Quakers*, *Shakers*, and *Muggletonians*. Thus, and by divers other Ways and subtil Devices, doth *Apollyon* and *Sin* invade, with their mighty Force and Militia of Hell, the Poor, Weak, and Feeble Inhabitants of the Country of *Non-Age*, till at last they come generally under the Education and Tutoring of one *Hate-Good*, who teaches them all her Hellish Mysteries; as to condemn all *Godly Counsel* and *Instructions*; nay, and to scoff, reproach, and jeer at all who are truly *Religious*; and not only to deride and flout at them,

but

The Progress of SIN: *Or,*

but to loll out their Tongues and point at them; and also to make and sing prophane and filthy Songs of them. But by the Providence of God, Two grave Matrons of good Parentage, being cast in amongst them, one called *Civility*, the other *Modesty*, both of the Town of *Morality*, who took the Charge and Care of Tutoring some of them, brought them up under very good *Discipline*, according to their *Light* and *Knowledge*. But these I hear too, when they came into *Youth-shire*, were utterly corrupted, spoiled, and overcome by the Power and Policy of this bloody Monster.

Yet, as God would have it, there was a few Honourable and High-born Worthies, who were sent on purpose by the *Prince of Light*, to Tutor some few of this young Progeny, or else the Enemy had made a perfect and compleat Conquest of them all. Their Names were *Christiana, True-Zeal, God-Fear, Special-Grace, Sobriety, Temperance*, and *Prudence*.

But *Sin* had got Tutors for most of them so soon, and so corrupted them, that they were gone out of the Country or State of *Non-Age*, and had took up Arms for *Apollyon*, before these Good and Virtuous Ladies came. I think it may not be amiss here, to give you two or three Instances of some that worsted and overcame this Hellish Tyrant.

One *Mary Warren*, Born in *May* 1651. Aged Ten Years, had a blessed Work of *Grace* upon her, and gave clear Evidence of a Victory she had got over *Sin* and *Satan*. Some asking her, *Whether she was willing to die?* She replied, *Aye, very willing, for then I shall sin no more: For I know that* Christ's *Blood hath made Satisfaction for my Sins.* At

At another Time, in her Sickness, she said, *That Satan stood at her Left side, and God was on er Right, and opened the Gates of Heaven for her; and Satan* (saith she) *shall not hurt me, tho' he sought to devour me like a roaring Lyon: Whether I live or die, it will be well with me;* God *is satisfy'd through his* Son Jesus Christ, *for he hath washed my Sins away in his Blood.*

Another Child, about Eleven Years Old, as she was Praying to this Effect; *That she might not look for any thing to rest on, or trust upon for Justification, whereby to stand Righteous before* God, *but only in* Jesus Christ *alone, who died for her at Jerusalem, and rose again the Third Day for her Justification.*

When Prayer was ended, she told her Father, *Now I believe in* Christ, *and am not afraid to die.*

Behold *Faith* in a *Babe* makes the Enemy fly.

Another poor Child that went a Begging from Door to Door, who lived in the Parish of *Newington-Butts:* This Boy was a very Moniter of Wickedness, for he would call filthy Names, Curse and Swear; yet a Gracious Man out of Pity took him as his own, and put him to be Educated by a godly Woman; and it is wonderful to hear what Power this poor Child got over *Sin* and his Master *Apollyon;* for in a little Time she taught him to Pray fervently, and to seek after the Knowledge of Jesus Christ: And he proved so good a Proficient, that he, with much Abhorrence, cry'd out on himself, not only for his Swearing, Lying, and other evil Vices he had been guilty of, but also was in great Horror for the Sin of his Nature, and Vileness

ness of his Heart. And he did not only Pray much himself, with strong Cries and Tears, but begged the Prayers of others for him. And at last (th. filled full of Doubts about his Eternal Estate) he came to take a little Hold of that Promise, *Come unto me all ye that are weary and heavy laden, and I will give you Rest.* But O! how did this poor Boy admire and bless God for the least Hopes, and at last came to great Satisfaction of his Interest in Christ, and Victory over his cursed Enemies, *Sin* and *Satan*; and remained in a Holy and Pious Frame, being filled with inward Joy, until he died.

I could give you several other Examples; but because some are not easily brought to believe such Things, I will say no more.

Yet, notwithstanding, tho' some few of this poor Progeny in the State of *Non-Age*, were thus enabled by good Education, and the Grace of God, to vanquish the cursed Enemy; yet what fearful Slaughter and Spoil did he make of the rest, *raging, raving*, and *roaring* about like a *hungry* and *greedy Lyon*; rending and tearing them in Pieces, not shewing any Pity, nor in the least regarding their tender Age: So that in every Town and City may be seen the sad Examples of his Conquest and merciless Cruelty, by their *Ignorance, Pride, Lying, Swearing, Stubbornness, Rebellion*, and all other *evil Habits Sin* has infused into them. So that we may say, with sorrowful Hearts, the Country of *Non-Age* is subdued, and brought under the Power and Kingdom of the *Prince of Darkness*: Most Parents bring up their Children to enlarge his Territories.

CHAP.

CHAP. V.

Shewing how Tyrant-Sin, in his Progress, Travelled into Youth-shire; and of the fearful Conquest and Slaughter he made there.

AFTER *Sin* had actually subdued the Country of *Non-Age*, like a cruel and Blood-thirsty Tyrant that delights in nothing but Rapine and Murder, he greedily follows his Prey; and therefore with great Speed, and no less Fury (*Apollyon* being enraged at the Loss he sustained, in not having made a perfect Conquest in the said Country) but contrariwise basely worsted by a few weak, contemptible Soldiers.

He in the next Place came into, and invaded the whole Country of *Youth-shire*, where dwells Abundance of Young Men and Maidens, some of which had cruel Marks on them of his former Conquest, when they remained in the Country of *Non-Age*; but by reason of those Reverend and Grave Matrons before-mentioned, divers of them being in this, as well as in those Regions, he was afraid of being supplanted; and therefore resolved not to lose those by Negligence, that he had beguiled and overcome by Craft and Subtilty: Nor was he quite without Hopes of re-gaining some in *Youth-shire*, which he had lost in the Country aforesaid: And observing many of the Inhabitants together, and perceiving their natural Inclinations, he salutes them after this Manner:

Gentlemen, *and you* Young Ladies: *Are you willing to entertain a* Traveller, *and walk a little Way with me?*

Upon

Upon this they all seemed at first to make a Pause, 'till one (whose wanton Looks betrayed the Inclinations of his Heart) answered, *Sir, What are you?*

Sin. Sir, I will assure you, no Enemy to those youthful Joys, Delights, *and* Pleasures *which your sweet and sprightly Nature is so much set upon; but I am he whom you stand in great want of, in order to the greatening, raising, and encreasing of your transcendent Happiness in this* World, *or making your Lives comfortable to you; for divers of you (I perceive) look sad and dejected, as if something troubled your Hearts, which I will teach you to cast at your Heels. If any of you will be Fools, and spend your Days in Sadness, who can help it? There is no need of it, if you will believe me; and I will assure you, Gentlemen, Millions in the World have, and still do, before such who talk of strange Joys and Delights, which are only fond Conceits of melancholy Fools, who prate of Things they never saw, and flatter themselves with a Crown of inconceivable Glory. These Things are Fancies, besides, suit not with your Natures; nor are they now presently to be had: If you will embrace me, and make me your Friend and Bosom-Companion, there's nothing which your Hearts can desire, but you shall have it: You that are for* Riches *shall have them; I will teach you rare Devices to catch them; tho' 'tis said,* They make themselves Wings and fly away; *yet I can tell you how to clip their Wings, and bring them with a Vengeance into your Coffers; so that you that are Gentlemen of mean Fortune, shall have no Cause to fear wanting Money to spend at* Taverns, *at* Games, *and* Whore-Houses, *for I am no Enemy to such fine Delights.*

You

You that are for Pleasures shall have your Fill; my Revels are opened to Chambering, Dancing, and Wantonness, Dice, Cards, and all Manner of Night-Sports; as, Kissing, Toying, and Courting, Hawking and Hunting, or whatsoever your Flesh best approves of: Gentlemen, you are welcome.

You that are for Honour, and would have your Names famous to Posterity, I will teach you the ready Way to attain it: Who was it raised the Renown of Nebuchadnezzar, Herod the Great, the Glorious Cæsar, and Mighty Mahomet? Did not I? If you be for Temporal Grandeur, 'tis I must mount you; and if for Spiritual Promotion, I can fit you: For who set the Triple Crown on Peter's Successor, but myself? If you are not willing without Advice to embrace me, go to Council; or would you have Examples, I have both ready.

For Counsellors, go to Mr. Carnal-Reason, Flesh and Blood, &c. whose Judgments are Grave and Solid, Safe and Harmless; if it was not so, do you think so many Thousands, and them of all sorts, and some of the wisest, would so readily receive it?

Ask your Five Senses, and they will tell you; ye have enough to advise with: And then, for Examples, they are innumerable; but be sure, do not mistake me; I include not Joseph, Moses, Obadiah, David, Daniel, John, nor Timothy, whom I hope you will not be such Fools to follow. But not to keep you in the Dark; there is all the Old World, and the greatest Part of this, whom if you imitate, I need proceed no further: If the Examples of Mighty Emperors, Famous Heroes, and many Noble Ones of the Earth, with the greatest Part of the Residue of Mankind, will not affect you; then let the Pattern of some of

your

72 The Progress of SIN: Or,

your Parents *and* Progenitors *be your* Copy; *nay*, *and call to mind your own* Experience: *Have you not already had a* Taste *of my* Dainties? *Do they not please your curious* Palates? *Do I offer* Things *unpleasant? All the Ways I lead in are strewed* Roses, *and perfumed with* Myrrh, Frankincense, Alloes, *and* Cinnamon: *What say you*, Sirs?

Upon this, smiling one upon another, one quickly broke Silence, and spoke to this Purpose:

Faith Lads, *this seems a brave jolly Fellow, he'll make Mirth for us, and be a fit Companion for such gallant Youngsters as we: Come, let's embrace him, and close with these* Suggestions: *Let's lay the Reins loose upon the Neck of our Lusts, and make him to chuse our Ways for us. But stay,* says another, *I fear he will make us meer* Spend-thrifts; *for I love not that wanton Fellow* Prodigality, *tho' he be in high Esteem now-a-days, and beloved of many Ladies for his good Gifts, and followed by many Rich Citizens Sons, who have raised his Grandeur by their Fathers Money, so as to purchase a Chariot for him; yet I have heard it is drawn by Four base Horses, viz.* Rashness, Luxury, Spend-all, *and* Folly; *his Coachman being the* Devil, *and one (whom I hate) called* Beggary, *rides behind. And tho' his Chariot runs a thundering Pace, and he seems secure, yet there's Abundance of Folks, as* Merchants, Mercers, Drapers, Silk-men *and* Taylors, *pursue him with cruel long Bills, so that for his Fooling he is like to pay dearly.*

Apollyon perceiving this Youth's Temper, whisper'd in *Peccatum*'s Ear, and said, *This Fellow will make a good Niggard.* And presently he put the Tyrant into another Habit; who at a convenient Time met him, to whom he did impart such rare

Stratagems

Stratagems how to grow *Rich*, and keep that which he had already gotten, which so won the *Young Duckworm's Heart*, that he joyfully embraced him.

What the Counsel was, seemed at first a Secret, but by his After-carriage and Behaviour it was guess'd at; for he became a *sneaking, lean, ill-fac'd, ink-belly'd Rascal*; grudging himself every Bit he eat, and fed much upon *Bread* and *Cheese, Red-Herrings*, &c. and oftentimes was seen to go to the *Pump* to drink his *Morning's Draught*: And in his Trading he pinch'd every Body in his *Weights* and *Measures*; and would not give or lend a Penny scarcely, tho' it was to keep his own Father out of Prison: And in Process of Time he became a great *Usurer*; where with his Bags of Gold and Silver we will leave him, and return to the other Company, who seeing which Way their Fellow was gone, fell all a laughing, and with cursed Oaths and taunting Expressions, reproached him 'cause he was not for *Rioting* and *Drunkenness, Chambering* and *Wantonness*; and yet, poor Soul, as much in the Tyrant's Chains as they. But hark! how they Sing and Carouse it, crying out to this deluding Tyrant, *We are your Servants, Sir*; *Hey Boys, One and All, One and All*; *let us cast away Sorrow from us, and take our Swing of Pleasures, and To-morrow shall be as this Day, and much more abundant.*

Stay, said one amongst them, *I am taken with a strange Trembling*; *I doubt 'tis an Enemy that thus doth court us, and that the whole Country is invaded*; *for somebody whispers strange Things in my Ears*; *sad Wars, doubtless, in me are approaching*; *for I was Educated by a most Noble, Virtuous Tutor, in the*

D   *Country*

Country of *Non-Age*, called *Civility*; who instructed me to fight against *Vice*, *Rioting*, and *Wantonness*; and told me of the Danger that was like to befal me as I passed through this Place. I must leave you, tho' it grieves me; my *Conscience* 'tis that gripes me: Hark! (said one of the jovial Company) what Fool have we here? *Conscience!* a *Fanatical Fancy!* why are you troubled? Because (said he) I fear this Traveller will debauch us; for I hear his Name is *Sin*, the bloody Tyrant, who destroyed almost all the Country from whence we came.

Sin seeing this, whisper'd one in the Ear, whose Name was *Shameless*, and said, Discourse with him, I will help you to Arguments, lest you lose him.

Shameless. His Name is *Sin*, you say: Is it an Evil to be merry, to drink a Glass of Wine or two with Good Fellows, and court a fair Lady? Do not these Things belong to our Age; and is it not the Fashion in all Countries amongst the greate Gallants? But if you will leave our Company, we will load you with *Reproach* and *Infamy*, that shall be harder for you to bear than the Name of *You Huff*, or *Spend-thrift*.

With that, a wanton Lass amongst them start up, and shamefully abused him, calling him Goodman *Shame-face*, and *Timorous*; and another took him about the Neck and kissed him; and with impudent Face, said to him, *Come, my Boy, stol'n Water is sweet, and Bread eaten in secret is pleasant. I have decked my Bed for thee with Coverings of Tapestry, with Carved Works, and Fine Linen of Egypt, and have perfumed it with Myrrh, Aloes and Cinnamon: Come, go along with me, and let us take our Fill of Love until Morning.* The poor Soul not being able longer to resist such powerful
Tem-

Temptations, nor endure their base Reproaches, was overcome by *Sin*, and straitway followed her, *as an Ox goes to the Slaughter, or as a Fool to the Correction of the Stocks, till a Dart struck through his Liver; as a Bird hasteth to the Snare, and knows not it is for his Life*. The jolly Company perceiving they had gained the Field, fell into a Laughter, triumphing in such Sort, with fearful *Damnings* and *Carousings*, as if the Day was their own, and in a little Time they should subdue all under *Apollyon*'s Scepter; so that for a great while nothing was heard but *Oaths* and *Blasphemy*; nor durst any gainsay them, for fear of being knocked down or stabbed; and upon this, *Sin* being flushed with Victory, ravaged all the Country of *Youth-shire*, Town and Family, Male and Female: And those he could not overcome by Pleasure, he overcame by Profit; and those that fell not by the Lust of the Flesh, fell by the Pride of Life; so that it would even melt a Heart of Stone to see what Desolation was made in every Corner, *Lust* prevailing and enlarging her Territories; *Youth* being so generally blinded by the Deceit of this Enemy and Impostor, who vauntingly displayed the Banner of *Luxury* and *Looseness* throughout the whole World, daily sending Millions out of this and other Places, to inhabit the great Country of *Sensuality*.

Thus by all Manner of *Debauchery* is the Country of *Youth-shire* spoiled by this cursed Enemy, and many Thousands of Young Men and Virgins made his professed Vassals, by being prostrated as a Prey to *Lust* and *Rapine*. Alas! how grievous is it to see such Stars of this lower Globe, and those the most Spangled, Bright, and Shining above many, as Roses amongst Lillies, or the Quintessence of Beauty obscured, eclipsed, and utterly stained and darkned, being led to *Dishonour*, ransacked of the *richest Dowry* of *Nature*, or robbed of that *invaluable Jewel* (I mean) their *Chastity*, even as a *Bee* of her *Sting*; left to bewail their Misery, and to curse those Tongues who drew them in, or beguiled them with their Golden Words, which gilded over those *bitter Pills* they have swallowed, and must vomit up again by *Repentance*, or perish for ever.

Apollyon and his Agent beholding the Victory they had gained in *Youth-shire*, thought now he should soon get his Regiments full, and so perfect what was wanting in these Parts, in order to a total Conquest; and indeed many Voluntiers daily Listed themselves to fight under the *Prince of Darkness*; some being allured by one Means, and some by another. But on a sudden the Leaders observed one throwing down his Arms, and running away, which caused great Confusion: One cryed, *Knock him down*; others, *Stab him*: And indeed, he w[as] on a sudden sadly wounded in his *Name*, being render'd as the vilest Wretch on Earth; but at last one of the jovial Boys, called *Impudence*, being stirred up by *Peccatum*, spoke to him to this Effect:

Impudence. Friend, What is the Cause you [de]sert us, and have thrown down your Arms?

Convert. (For that it seems was his Name,) [I] am convinced that the Ways you go in are evil and very dangerous; and that this *Traveller* whom you have entertained, is the *King's Enemy*, nay, most *bloody* and *cruel Traytor*; and therefore I a[m] resolved to be gone, and obtain a *Pardon*, if pos[si]ble, for what is past.

Impu.

Stratagems how to grow *Rich*, and keep that which he had already gotten, which so won the *Young Auckworm's Heart*, that he joyfully embraced him. What the Counsel was, seemed at first a Secret, but by his After-carriage and Behaviour it was guess'd at; for he became a *sneaking, lean, ill-fac'd, ink-belly'd Rascal*; grudging himself every Bit he eat, and fed much upon *Bread* and *Cheese*, *Red-Herrings*, &c. and oftentimes was seen to go to the *Pump* to drink his *Morning's Draught*: And in his Trading he pinch'd every Body in his *Weights* and *Measures*; and would not give or lend a Penny scarcely, tho' it was to keep his own Father out of Prison: And in Process of Time he became a great *Usurer*; where with his Bags of Gold and Silver we will leave him, and return to the other Company, who seeing which Way their Fellow was gone, fell all a laughing, and with cursed Oaths and taunting Expressions, reproached him 'cause he was not for *Rioting* and *Drunkenness*, *Chambering* and *Wantonness*; and yet, poor Soul, as much in the Tyrant's Chains as they. But hark! how they Sing and Carouse it, crying out to this deluding Tyrant, *We are your Servants, Sir*; *Hey Boys, One and All, One and All; let us cast away Sorrow from us, and take our Swing of Pleasures, and To-morrow shall be as this Day, and much more abundant.*

Stay, said one amongst them, *I am taken with a strange Trembling*; *I doubt 'tis an Enemy that thus doth court us, and that the whole Country is invaded*; *for somebody whispers strange Things in my Ears; sad Wars, doubtless, in me are approaching; for I was Educated by a most Noble, Virtuous Tutor, in the*

D   *Country*

Country of *Non-Age*, called *Civility*; who instructed me to fight against *Vice*, *Rioting*, and *Wantonness*; and told me of the Danger that was like to befa[l] me as I passed through this Place. I must leave you, tho' it grieves me; my *Conscience* 'tis tha[t] gripes me: Hark! (said one of the jovial Company what Fool have we here? *Conscience!* a *Fanatica[l] Fancy!* why are you troubled? Because (said he) [I] fear this Traveller will debauch us; for I hear his Name is *Sin*, the bloody Tyrant, who destroyed almost all the Country from whence we came.

Sin seeing this, whisper'd one in the Ear, whos[e] Name was *Shameless*, and said, Discourse with him, I will help you to Arguments, lest you lose him.

Shameless. His Name is *Sin*, you say: Is it a[n] Evil to be merry, to drink a Glass of Wine or two with Good Fellows, and court a fair Lady? D[o] not these Things belong to our Age; and is it [in] the Fashion in all Countries amongst the great[e] Gallants? But if you will leave our Company, [we] will load you with *Reproach* and *Infamy*, that sh[all] be harder for you to bear than the Name of *You[ng] Huff*, or *Spend-thrift*.

With that, a wanton Lass amongst them sta[rt] up, and shamefully abused him, calling him Goo[d] man *Shame-face*, and *Timorous*; and another [flew] him about the Neck and kissed him; and with [an] impudent Face, said to him, *Come, my Boy, stol[en] Water is sweet, and Bread eaten in secret is pleasa[nt], I have decked my Bed for thee with Coverings of Ta[pestry, with Carved Works, and Fine Linen o[f] Egypt, and have perfumed it with Myrrh, Aloe[s] and Cinnamon: Come, go along with me, and let [us] take our Fill of Love until Morning.* The po[or] Soul not being able longer to resist such powerf[ul]

Temptations, nor endure their base Reproaches, was overcome by *Sin*, and straitway followed her, *as an Ox goes to the Slaughter, or as a Fool to the Correction of the Stocks, till a Dart struck through his Liver; as a Bird hasteth to the Snare, and knows not it is for his Life*. The jolly Company perceiving they had gained the Field, fell into a Laughter, triumphing in such Sort, with fearful *Damnings* and *Carousings*, as if the Day was their own, and in a little Time they should subdue all under *Apollyon*'s Scepter; so that for a great while nothing was heard but *Oaths* and *Blasphemy*; nor durst any gainsay them, for fear of being knocked down or stabbed; and upon this, *Sin* being flushed with Victory, ravaged all the Country of *Youth-shire*, Town and Family, Male and Female: And those he could not overcome by Pleasure, he overcame by Profit; and those that fell not by the Lust of the Flesh, fell by the Pride of Life; so that it would even melt a Heart of Stone to see what Desolation was made in every Corner, *Lust* prevailing and enlarging her Territories; *Youth* being so generally blinded by the Deceit of this Enemy and Impostor, who vauntingly displayed the Banner of *Luxury* and *Looseness* throughout the whole World, daily sending Millions out of this and other Places, inhabit the great Country of *Sensuality*.

Thus by all Manner of *Debauchery* is the Country of *Youth-shire* spoiled by this cursed Enemy, and many Thousands of Young Men and Virgins made his professed Vassals, by being prostrated as a Prey to *Lust* and *Rapine*. Alas! how grievous it to see such Stars of this lower Globe, and those the most Spangled, Bright, and Shining above many, as Roses amongst Lillies, or the Quintessence of Beauty obscured, eclipsed, and utterly stained and darkned, being led to *Dishonour*, ransacked of the *richest Dowry of Nature*, or robbed of that *invaluable Jewel* (I mean) their *Chastity*, even as a *Bee* of her *Sting*; left to bewail their Misery, and to curse those Tongues who drew them in, or beguiled them with their Golden Words, which gilded over those *bitter Pills* they have swallowed, and must vomit up again by *Repentance*, or perish for ever.

Apollyon and his Agent beholding the Victory they had gained in *Youth-shire*, thought now he should soon get his Regiments full, and so perfect what was wanting in these Parts, in order to a total Conquest; and indeed many Voluntiers daily Listed themselves to fight under the *Prince of Darkness*; some being allured by one Means, and some by another. But on a sudden the Leaders observed one throwing down his Arms, and running away, which caused great Confusion: One cryed, *Knock him down*; others, *Stab him*: And indeed, he was on a sudden sadly wounded in his *Name*, being render'd as the vilest Wretch on Earth; but at last one of the jovial Boys, called *Impudence*, being stirred up by *Peccatum*, spoke to him to this Effect:

Impudence. Friend, What is the Cause you desert us, and have thrown down your Arms?

Convert. (For that it seems was his Name,) I am convinced that the Ways you go in are evil and very dangerous; and that this *Traveller* whom you have entertained, is the *King's Enemy*, nay, most *bloody* and *cruel Traytor*; and therefore I am resolved to be gone, and obtain a *Pardon*, if possible, for what is past.   *Impu-*

Impudence. Sirrah, Who is your *Tutor?*

Convert. A very virtuous Lady, whose Name is *Christiana.*

Impudence. What Lessons hath she taught you?

Convert. Very good Ones.

1. To find more Sweetness in leaving *Sin*, than ever I found in the committing of it.

2. To leave and loath every *Sin*, because 'tis so hateful to *God*, and contrary to his *Nature*, and *Holy Law*.

3. To live a *Holy Life*, and do much Good; and to make but little Noise of it.

4. To prefer the *Duty* I owe, above the *Danger* I fear.

5. How to sacrifice a stout and stubborn Will for *God's Honour*, rather than to do the Devil a Pleasure.

6. To bring up the Bottom of my *Life* to the Top of my *Light*; and that I should not sin against my *Light*, lest I sin away my *Life*.

7. To chuse rather to be saved in a *rough Sea*, than to be drowned in a *calm River*.

8. To bear the *Cross for Christ*, in *suffering*, lest I lose the *Crown of Christ*, by *sinning*.

9. Likewise, to chuse rather to be afflicted with *Lazarus* on Earth, than to be tormented with *Dives* in Hell.

10. And to leave that *Company* here, that would bring my *Soul* to Destruction hereafter.

11. Also to chuse the worst of *Sorrow* before the least *Sin*; because there is more Evil in that, than there is in the greatest Affliction.

12. To mourn most for those *Sins* before *God*, that appear least before *Men*; for the outward *Acts* are more scandalous, yet inward *Lusts* are more dangerous. 13. Hereby

13. Hereby she taught me to be better inwardly in *Substance*, than outwardly in *Appearance*; for those who deceive others with the false *Shew* of *Holiness*, deceive themselves with the false *Hope* of *Happiness*.

14. To desire *Grace* not only to be saved, but also to be sanctified; and to endeavour to have *Sin Crucified*, as well as *Pardoned*; and to be made *Holy* on *Earth*, as well as *Happy* in *Heaven*.

15. To undertake all *Christian Duties*, yet wholly to rely upon *God's Mercies*; or to be much for *Doing*, and yet seek to be saved only in a Way of *Believing*.

16. To speak well of what *God* is, and to think well of what *God* does; and never to complain of the Badness of the *Times* and *Seasons*, if I can but get *God* to be my *Portion*.

17. To be more in Love with the *God* of the *Altar*, than with the *Gold* of the *Altar*; or to covet as much the *God* of *Mercies*, as the *Mercies* of *God*.

18. To look more at Home than Abroad, how 'tis with me, than how 'tis with others; and that the readiest Way to know whether or no I am in *Christ*, is to know whether *Christ* is in me; because the *Fruit* is more visible than the *Root*.

19. To set out for *God* in my *Beginning*, and hold out with *God* unto my *Ending*; and that the best Way to have the whole *Harvest* of our *Lives* sanctified by him, is to have the *First* of our *Lives* dedicated to him; who prizes more the Blossom of *Youth*, than the Sheddings of *Old Age*.

20. To value the *Joys* of *Heaven*, above the *Vanities* of the *Earth*.

The Travels *of* Ungodliness. 79

21. She taught me also to remember, That whatsoever I do on *Earth*, 'tis eyed by the *God of Heaven*; and that after all my *present Receivings*, there will come a Time of *future Reckonings*. Besides that there is no obtaining what is promised, without doing what is commanded; and that *Inward Purity* is the ready Way to *Eternal Plenty*.

22. Moreover, That all the Time that *God* allows us on *Earth*, is little enough to do that *Work God* allots us: And that 'tis my chiefest Business to make sure of *Future Blessedness*.

Lastly, That I should sow such *Seed* whilst I live, as I would be glad to eat the *Fruit* of when I die.

Upon this, *Impudence* swore he would tread him and his *Tutor* under his Feet, if he would not return back.

But *Apollyon* seeing that Force would do no Good, raised up another, whose Name was *Self-Conceit*, to dispute and reason out the Case with him.

Self Conceit. Brother, what is the Cause you are so strangely alter'd of late, and have forsaken our Company?

Convert. Because I see the Way is dangerous in which you go; you are all blinded in taking this Traveller *Peccatum* for a Friend, for he secretly designs (I hear) to murder you all. Do you not read in the *Bible*, what Work *Sin* has made in the World?

Self-Conceit. You mistake yourself, and think that is *Sin*, which is not: Don't think the *Golden Cup* of *Profit*, *Pleasures*, and *Honours*, are such frightful Things.

Convert. Friend, You see the *Bait*, but not the *Hook*; the *Golden Cup*, but not the *Poison* in it: You taste the *Sweet* of *Sin* now, but see not the

D 4 bitter

bitter *Wrath* and *Misery* that follows it. You are like our *First Parents*, that this Enemy cheated, who took an *Apple* in Exchange for a *Paradise*. For my Part, I will not any longer play like a silly *Fish* with this *Angler's Bait*. What is the *Pleasure* of *Sin* here, when weighed against the *Pain* for it hereafter? The *Sweet* will soon be gone, but the *Bitter* will last for ever. This Enemy is a *Deceiver*; whilst he kisses the *Lips*, he betrays the *Soul* into the Hands of the *Devil*. Therefore tempt me not, for I cannot stand under the *Guilt* of the least *Iniquity*.

The Company seeing they could not prevail with him to return, abused him most fearfully, calling him at their Pleasure. But one of the Youths observing that *Convert* had clearly worsted them, was mightily wrought upon, and he was resolved to leave them too; which made *Apollyon* grind his Teeth, and foam dreadfully. But all was in vain; for God had opened his Eyes and Mouth to speak to this Purpose:

Illuminatus. (For so was he called.) Good Brother, How did you get Power over this cursed *Peccatum*, and the *Prince of Darkness*? I am persuaded thou art that Young Man that I have read of in a little Book, called, *War with the* Devil.*

Convert. Thou say'st right; I am that Person.

Illum. Why then, I understand by that the Course you took; and by the Help of God, I will go on in the same Way. I perceive *Conscience* was a great Friend to you.

Convert. Yes, when he was rightly informed, or had his Eyes enlightened by God's Word, he proved useful

Sold by W. Johnston, *in* Ludgate-Street

The Travels of Ungodliness. 81

useful to me: But he could do nothing to purpose, till the Spirit and Grace of God was infused into my Soul.

Illum. I have had great Sorrow upon my Heart for my abominable Sins, since I have read concerning your Conversion. But I cannot believe.

Convert. You must cry to God as I did for Faith, and ponder well the Promises of God; for I am persuaded thou wilt meet with a sharp Conflict: And indeed so it fell out. For

Apollyon set upon him most furiously: And not knowing but it may be of Use to some, we will give you an Account of his Combat with him.

Apol. You have been a very great Sinner in entertaining this Traveller, who is a cruel Enemy to God; and now there is no Ground to think God will forgive you, for his Wrath will overtake you suddenly.

Illum. The Storm of God's Wrath, Satan, is over in Christ; he declares, *He is merciful, and will not keep his Anger for ever*, Jer. iii. 12.

Apol. But alas! you are ignorant of God and Christ, and he will take Vengeance on all such: Doth not the Scripture say so?

Illum. But Satan, God has promised to *Lead the Blind*, &c. In another Place, *He calls simple Ones, and those that have no Understanding*, Prov. i. 21, 22.

Apol. But your Heart is hard and obdurate, you know not the Vileness of it; there is not a filthier Creature under the Heavens; and therefore you are certainly an undone Man.

Illum. But God has promised to give me a Heart of Flesh, and take away my stony Heart; and if I loath myself for my Vileness, he hath promised

D 5

to wash and cleanse me from all my Sins, *Ezek.* xx. xliii. xxxvi. and xxvi.

Apol. But you have been as wicked as you could well be, and therefore are a damned Creature.

Illum. Aye, Satan, I cannot deny that, but yet God hath promised Mercy and Pardon to such who have spoken and done as evil Things as they could; and therefore there is Hope for me. *Jer.* iii. 5.

Apol. But all this while you do but compliment with me: You do not think indeed, there is Mercy for you in God's Heart.

Illum. I do not compliment, thou lyest in that; tho' I cannot deny but I have through thy Temptations, been so foolish to think so indeed. But God saith, *His Thoughts are not my Thoughts*. And hath also said, *He will abundantly pardon me, if I turn from my evil Ways*, Isaiah lv. 6, 7, 8. therefore 'tis no Matter what my Thoughts have been.

Apol. But for all this, I shall be too hard for thee, and break thy Head e'er I have done.

Illum. No, the Promise runs, *You shall but bruize my Heel.*

Apol. Aye, but you forget your abominable Sins: Remember the fearful lewd Life you have lived.

Illum. Christ died for Sinners, and I fly to him.

Apol. But you have sinned against Light and Knowledge.

Illum. What though, I am but a Sinner, Satan, notwithstanding, and Christ died for Sinners.

Apol. But you cannot Believe; you are guilty of that Sin: And he hath said, *Such who Believe not, shall be Damned.*

Illum. But Satan, if I can't Believe, yet I may Believe; God can give me Faith; and tho' I am

now

The Travels *of* Ungodliness.   83

now an Unbeliever, and so the worst of Sinners, yet I am but a Sinner, and Christ died for Sinners, nay, for the chiefest of Sinners; and therefore I will not give up my Hope yet.

Apol. Hope! You have no Ground for Hope.

Illum. No, Satan; that is false, I am sure: Is not Christ's Death a Ground, nay, a good Ground for Hope? *Who shall condemn? It is Christ that died,* Rom. viii. 34. On his Blood and Merits I will rely.

Apol. What Good can his Death do thee? How can he save thee, who could not save himself? It brought him to the Grave.

Illum. Thou cursed Blasphemer! He laid down his Life freely, (none took it from him) to satisfy God's Justice, and rose again from the Dead the Third Day; and thereby triumphed over Thee, and all the *Powers of Darkness*: And is not his Resurrection a good Ground for Hope?

Apol. But I do accuse thee, and will plead against thee; because thou hast been so long my Servant, and an Enemy to him.

Illum. I matter not that; thou art a vile Deceiver: The other Day thou didst endeavour to persuade me my Sins were small, and that God would pardon them at any Time: And are they now so great and foul, that Christ's Blood cannot wash them away? What care I tho' thou do'st plead against me, since Jesus Christ pleads for me? Is not the Intercession of Christ for Transgressors a good Ground of Hope?

Apol. Thou hast no Grace, or not enough to bear you up in the Day of Trial; and therefore thy State is very sad.

Illum. Christ hath Grace enough, and I depend

D 6   not

84 *The* Progress *of* SIN: *Or,*

not upon the Grace that is in Me; but on that Grace which is in Him: He is full of Grace, and 'tis in Him, that it might be communicated to all such as I am. And is not here a good Ground of Hope?

Apol. Thou wilt fall into Sin again, at some Time or another, and I shall devour thee.

Illum. God has promised in his Blessed Covenant, That *Sin shall not have Dominion over us,* Rom. vi. 14. and, That he will put his *Fear so into our Hearts, that we shall not depart from him,* Jer. xxxii. 39. And is not his Covenant a good Ground for Hope? Nay, and he hath said, That he will bruize thee under my Feet shortly.

Moreover, He has promised, *He will uphold me:* And Christ hath pray'd, *That my Faith fail not;* and I am sure, He was heard; because he has confirmed all his Promises by an Oath: And is not here good Ground for me to hope, He that hath begun a *Good Work in me, will perform it to the Day of Christ,* Phil. i. 6.

Apol. Thou art an Hypocrite.

Illum. 'Tis the *Father of Lies* that says it. 'Is there any Sin that I have not been humbled for, and forsaken? Do I not desire to be Holy as well as Happy? Satan, I fear nor hate nothing more than Hypocrisy, and therefore am no Hypocrite: But if I am an Hypocrite, I am but a Sinner; and *Christ died for Sinners;* and all *Sins against Father, and Son, shall be forgiven to Men.* But I am no Hypocrite, because all the Faculties of my Soul are in Arms against Sin, and against it universally; against the Least, as well as the Greatest.

Apol. I will cause strange Evils to befal thee.

Illum.

Illum. All Things shall *work together for my Good*, *I love God*, Rom. iii. 28. And tho' I lose my life for Christ's Sake, I shall find it: When the torm comes, I will fly to Him.

Apol. Thou canst not go to God as a Saint; for thou art none.

Illum. I will go to him then as a Sinner; for that I am, thou say'st: And there are as many Promises of Mercy and Pardon made to Sinners, as Sinners, as are made to Saints, as such.

Apol. Would I could tear thee in Pieces, and devour thee at once, thou vile Enemy: Thou hast done, and wilt do me a great Mischief: All my Plagues light upon thee.

Illum. What, Satan, are you angry? Alas for you! 'Tis not *All you would*, but *All you may*, devour: Blessed be God, you cannot prevail against me.

By this Time by the *Shield of Faith*, he so stoutly resisted *Apollyon*, that he suddenly fled, and left the Young Man Master of the Field.

But this so enraged the Enemy, that he made fearful Work amongst the rest of the poor Inhabitants; so that except this *Youth*, and a few more, all generally in *Youth-shire*, were put, as it were, to the Sword. So that all the Country lay bleeding or weltring in their Blood, being fearfully mangled by the Hands of this merciless Monster, and cursed Traveller, *Sin*. So that, come where you would, in City and Country, you could hear of nothing hardly but horrid Oaths, cursing and Swearing, Whoring and Damning, as if Hell had been broke loose. Also, in most Places and Company, where they came, those who would not run with them to the same Excess of Riot, were their

meer

86 *The Progress of* SIN: *Or,*

meer Sport and Songs; every one striving to out-do his Fellow, and so be, as it were, the Captain-General under *Apollyon, Prince of Darkness;* who was not content to Fight with one Weapon only, by which he slew most, *viz.* by *Fleshly Lusts* and *Debauchery*; but also introduced many abominable Errors and pernicious Heresies, which destroyed divers others who had escaped the gross Pollutions of the World.

CHAP. VI.

Shewing how Tyrant-Sin *Travelled, into the vast Country, called* Sensuality; *wherein is discovered the* Nature, Manners, *and* strange Customs *of the* Inhabitants: *Together with the* Strength, Government, Trade, *and other* Rarities *found in a great City Situated in the same Regions; and of the prodigious and shameful Pranks he played there: Also, shewing the Manner how Three of the* Inhabitants *thereof made their Escape out of the said City and Country.*

THE Unweary Traveller, and Cursed Enemy, Sin, (having passed through, and near quite overcome and laid waste, the Country of *Non-Age* and *Youth-shire*) thought now he had sufficient stored the Country of *Sensuality* with Inhabitants; and therefore was resolved to Travel again into those Parts, and give them a fresh Visit. But before we relate any thing concerning his Projects here, it may not be amiss to give you a Descrip-

The Travels of Ungodliness. 87

...n of the Country, with the Nature, Manners, ...d Customs of the Inhabitants.

First, Then you must know, that this Country ...very large, (it is indeed the biggest Continent in ...he whole World) the Latitude, Longitude, and ...whole Circumference thereof is wonderful, and amazing to think upon: For, in this Country lies the greatest Part of *Muscovy*, *Tartary*, with the vast Empire of *Mahomet*, or Kingdom of *Turky*, *Prester John's Land*, with the biggest Part of *America*, and the *East* and *West-Indies*: Also, in some Parts and Confines thereof, lies the great City *Babylon*, containing divers mighty Streets; with Spiritual *Sodom* and *Egypt*, where our Lord was Crucified. Moreover, There is also a City which bears the same Name the Country doth; of which we shall hereafter speak more particularly.

Now, as touching the Inhabitants, the like you have hardly ever heard of: For this Bloody Tyrant, *Sin*, it seems, had formerly been amongst them; and by his Devilish Art and Subtilty, had so strangely Metamorphosed the People, that they are not at all (in many Respects) like rational Creatures; for they appear to have no more Reason than the Beasts that perish; nay, and are so far degenerated from what once they were, for some of them (I find in Holy Writ) look like *Lyons*, others like *Dragons*, *Dogs*, *Tygers*, *Bulls*, *Wolves*, *Swine*, *Serpents*, *Foxes*, &c. and many of them like *Asses*; and also act the Parts of all these Sorts of Animals.

There is one Thing more to be noted, which is, 'They are so mangled and slaughter'd by *Sin*, that some have no Eyes to see, nor Ears to hear, what
God

God by his Word or Works declares; nay, all their Spiritual Senses are quite lost, and their very Hearts and Consciences are defiled; so that from the Crown of their Heads, to the Soles of their Feet, there is nothing but Wounds and Bruises, and putrifying Sores. Moreover, the Enemy hath stript them of all Soul-Raiment and Ornaments; that in the Sight of him who hath Internal Eyes, they appear as Naked as ever a Child did, New-Born; and yet they are so deluded, that there is not One in Twenty of them ashamed: What Cover any have, is but like unto filthy Rags, or a menstruous Cloth, or those Cloths that are taken off of old Ulcers, or filthy running and stinking Sores; and yet some of them vaunt themselves in Pride, and spot their Faces, as if they were peerless for Beauty.

But possibly some may enquire, What Food the Country does afford? I cannot, alas! but pity them upon that very Account, for the Soil is very Barren; for the Native Growth, or Product of the Country is such, that it yields no Food for their Souls but *Ashes*, *Husks*, *Chaff*, and *Gravel-stones*; only some of the *Asses* feed upon the Wind, and snuff up the *East-Wind*.

If you search Sacred Records, you will find 'tis really so: Doth not the Scripture say, *The Wicked feed on Ashes, and Chaff, and the Wind?* What far Country was it that the *Prodigal Son* went into? And what *Citizen* was that, but *Satan*, whose *Swine* he fed with, and fain would have filled his Belly with the *Husks* they did eat? What are all the *Pleasures*, *Honours*, and *Riches* of the World, but as *Chaff*, compared with the *Dainties* of our *Father's House?* Thus

The Travels of Ungodliness.

Thus I have given you a brief Account of the monstrous Dispositions and Customs of the People of this great Country; where many live in Honour, and understand not, and therefore are said to be *like the Beasts that perish*: And I am sure you cannot go amongst them, but you will find (if you have not lost your Reason with them) these Things so. Alas! how like fat and pamper'd Horses do some of them appear, *Every one* (as the Prophet says) *neighing after his Neighbour's Wife*.

But, since I told you of the City *Sensuality*, that lies just as you enter into the Country, it is needful to speak first of the *Gate*, which is so exceeding wide, that Ten Thousand may go in together with much Ease: Yet 'tis divided into Five Divisions, that is, The *Five Senses*; and the Way to it seems (to *Fools*) to be strewed with *Roses*: And before the Great *Gate* is all manner of Fleshly Allurements to entice Travellers; for there stands a Multitude of fair Ladies, some with *Spotted Faces*, *Naked Breasts* and *Shoulders*, *Rolling* and *Wanton Eyes*; so that the Simple cannot but be taken with the Sight. And then, to please another of the *Five Senses*, they are very gentle, and as willing to come to Hand, and be play'd with, as ever was *Joseph's* Mistress.

Also there stands continually at the *Gate*, the *Waits* of the *City*, with all Sorts of rare and Flesh-ravishing Musick, that makes such a melodious Sound, that the Ear is engaged presently.

And then, for the Sense of *Smelling*, there are the rare Perfumes of the East, *Myrrh*, *Aloes* and *Frankincense*.

For *Tasting*; You have a Company of Good Fellows,

90 The Progress of SIN: Or,

The vast City of Sensuality
Apolions Castel

...ws, standing with Bottles of the best Spiced Wine, ...andy, and Tankards of Ale and Beer in their ...nds; saying, *Here is your rare Bub; come, let's ...ink, Carouse, and be Merry.* You may have ...o for your Money, the most delicious Food that ...e World affords: A Breakfast of the best Sort ...dear; but according to your Purse or Pocket, ...d Gluttonous Appetites, you may be accommo...ted, provided you will Eat and Drink to Excess; ...or otherwise there is no Entrance for you at this ...ate: From whence you may gather, the Inhabi...nts have not lost the Senses of the Body, though ...ey have the Spiritual Senses of the Soul.

But to proceed: The *Gate* that lets into the ...ty, hath Three Steps ascending: The First is, ...e *Conception of Lust*; the Second is, the *Sweet ...d Flesh-pleasing Contemplation* thereof; The Third ...e *Free Consent, and yielding* thereto; which no ...oner you get upon, but you are in the City.

Also, you must know, the Strength of the Place ...very great: It hath Three exceeding High and ...npregnable Walls. The First is, *Blindness of ...ind*; The Second is, *Presumption*; The Third, ...belief.

Under the Wall lies a wonderful deep and dan...erous Ditch, or Moat; which if any of the In...abitants, who by striving to get out of the City, ...ance to fall into, 'tis a Thousand to One, if ...ey ever get out again.

The Watch that keeps the Gate, is Six, with ...vers Infernal Spirits, all well armed: Insomuch, ...at without infinite Power there is no escaping.

At the farther End of the City is a Gate also, ...wide as the other, which stands always open: ...e Porter's Name is *Death*. More-

Moreover, behind that Gate is an exceeding deep Lake, that sends forth nothing but a Black Sulphurous Smoke of Fire and Brimstone: A[nd] all that Die in this City *Sensuality*, go out at th[is] Gate, and so fall into the Lake, which burns mo[re] fierce than Mount *Ætna*, or *Strombalo*.

In the Heart of the Town is a strong and wo[n]derful Castle, where *Apollyon* keeps his Court which is called *Hardness of Heart*. And one grea[t] Thing Tyrant *Sin* is employed about, is, to [bring] all the Inhabitants one after another gradually, a[s] they enter the City, into this Castle.

He that is Keeper of the Castle, is one *Obstinate* a very impudent and grim Fellow.

The Walk or Path to the Castle is pleasa[nt] enough; but at the Entrance of the Gate is Fo[ur] Steps, very fair to set your Feet upon: The F[irst] is called *Extenuation of Sin*; to make great Si[ns] small, and little Sins to seem none at all. Th[e] Second, To make Excuses about it, *viz. I wa[s] drawn in, My Heart is good, &c.* The Thir[d] Step is called, *Delight in Sin*; and from hence 't[is] defended, and pleaded for, by such who get u[p] thus high. The Fourth and last Step is, *Fin[al] Impenitency*; then you are in the Castle, and a[re] made Free Citizens; having a Right to all th[e] Privileges and Immunities, Trade and Traffic[k] thereof.

On one Side of the City, towards a Town cal[l]ed *Religion*, is a little Gate, so straight, that bu[t] a very few can get through: 'Tis called *Regenera[-]tion*; and he that opens it, hardly One in a Thou[-]sand who dwells in the City, knows; whose Nam[e] is *Repentance*.

Mor[e]

The Travels of Ungodliness. 93

Moreover, You must know, that in this City
[they] keep every Day a great Market, where
[one] exposeth to Sale divers very rich Commodities
[on] easy Terms.

For First, Here you may buy *Modesty* of some,
[w]hich is a choice Thing, for a *Toy* or two: The
[sa]me Commodity you may have of others for a
[b]are *Antick Fashion*, which, like Shop-Windows,
[m]ake a Shew of a *richer Jewel* to be had upon rea-
[s]onable Terms within.

2. Say what you will, *Chastity* is sold at this
Market very cheap.

3. There is to be sold those excellent Pearls of
[Tem]perance and *Sobriety*, for the Value of one Quart
[of] good Canary; or rather than fail, for a Dozen
[of] Beer or Ale, or for a Pint of Brandy; and the
[Per]son so well contented, that he matters not,
[if] he spue and wallow in his Filth like a drunken
[Swi]ne, to confirm the Bargain.

[4.] Here is also to be sold a Thing called *Truth*,
[or] *Honest-Dealing*, for the Gain of a Penny, if
[not] a Farthing. Such is their Love of Money.

5. And a *Good Conscience*, if there is any such
[Co]mmodity in the whole Town, is to be sold at
[the] very same Price. *The Love of Money is the*
[Roo]*t of all Evil.*

[6.] *Peace and Tranquility of Mind* on as easy
[ea]sy Terms, if it be possible to find it amongst
[t]hem.

7. Which is more than all the rest, *God, Christ*,
[an]d all the *Blessings purchased by* (the Price of) *his*
[mo]*st precious Blood*, with all the Inconceivable Pri-
[vi]leges of the *Gospel*, are not esteemed by most
[of] the Inhabitants of the City *Sensuality*, worth

one

94 *The* Progress *of* SIN: Or,

one *Lust*; and therefore let them but *Drink*, *Damn*, *Swear*, and *Whore*, and let who will take all such Things, with *Heaven* itself, &c.

But to proceed: In this City *Sin* also keeps School: (You must needs think the People are Educated with a Vengeance who have such a Tutor.) But pray be pleased to hear what rare Arts they are which he instructs them in.

1. He teaches all that are willing to learn of him, the deep Art of *Witchcraft* and *Conjuration*; but that is upon dear Terms.

2. He teaches the Art of *Swearing*, with all its Attendants.

3. The Art of *Drunkenness* and *Gluttony*, viz. How to drink Wine and strong Liquors abundantly; and to dress Meat, on purpose to provoke and make Provision for the Flesh.

4. The Art of *Ambition*, or *sinful Grandeur*.

5. The Art of *Covetousness*, a great Mystery, for (if well learned) thou mayest be as greedy Curmudgeon as any lives, and yet go for a liberal Person.

6. Here is taught also the curious Art of *Bravery* that is, All the newest, neatest, and most rare Fashions, that can be had for Love or Money; but chiefly those which tend to stir up to *Wantonness*, *Lust*, and *lascivious Embraces*; some of which you have heard already; but not only for the Body, but for your Houses, and all Things else.

7. The delicate Art of *Painting*, or *Beautifying* the *Skin*, *Face*, *Hands* and *Hair*; as the colouring the *Eye-brows*, clapping on a false and lying Blush on the *Cheeks*; and to change the very natural Colour of the *Hair*; nay, and to adulterate

he true and naked Complexion of the whole
 Head and Face.

. The mysterious Art of *Perfuming*, not only
 Hair, but the *Skin*, *Cloaths*, *Bedding*, *Linen*,
 Woollen, on purpose to stir up *Lust*, and so
 up the Trade of the City.

. The Art of *Whoring*; and the Truth is,
 is being a great Part of the City-Trade, *Apollyon*,
 seems, takes great Care to instruct these Sort of
 alers, that they might be better Proficients, if
 ible, than many others: Some he directs to
 with *impudent Faces* at their Doors, in the
 light, bravely garnished in *Silk Gowns*, &c.
 tho' it be known what they are, yet they are
 but laughed at: The Tradesmen in other Ci-
 at Night shut up their Shops, but these then
 theirs: When other Persons Trade is over,
 trumpet's Trade begins: She is set on Work,
 maintained perhaps, by those that undo the
 . Give Thanks, *O wide-mouth'd Hell*;
 Lucifer at this; and dance for Joy, all ye
 ls!

 t this Sort, very likely, take up their Dwel-
 n the Out-parts: But there are others who
 aught to Trade more secretly, and for fear,
 some People who like not this Vice, should
 them in Derision, *Apollyon*, to prevent their
 g discovered, teaches them to manage their
 rks of Darkness subtilly, after this Manner:
 f *Gallants* haunt the House where she is, then
 is taught to say, She is a Captain's Wife, or
 like, that is gone to the Wars in another
 try; and they come with Letters from her
 and. If *Merchants* resort to her, then to
                                    house

hoise up these Sails; That she is Wife to a Master of a Ship, and they bring News that her Husband is put in at the *Straights*, or *Venice*, or *Constantinople*, or at *Alexandria*, or *Scanderoon*. If *Shop-Keepers* come to her, why then she has bough[t] some Goods newly of them, and they come f[or] their Money. But if the Stream runs low, and none but *Apron-Lads* and *Journeymen* launch forth, then she keeps a Politick *Sempstress's-Shop*; and she sells or starches their Linen: And a Multitude of such Devices 'tis reported they have.

10. Here is taught also the Art of *Cheati*[ng] *Picking* and *Stealing*.

11. The Craft of *Lying*, *Dissembling*, and *Eq*[ui]*vocating*.

12. To omit many more; as, the Art of *S*[cof]*fing*, *Reproaching*, and *Villifying Virtue*; here taught the mysterious Art of *Atheism*. And if [you] please to read that most Excellent Book, writ [by] Sir *Charles Wolsey*, well worthy of perusing, [you] may see what a kind of Catechism the *Atheists* tea[ch.]

13. Here is also taught the Black and Hel[lish] Art of *Incest*, *Sodomy*, and all manner of *Be*[stial] and *Unnatural Lusts*.

14. The Art of *Sports*; or all manner of [un]*lawful Games*.

15. The Art of *Mirth*, *Musick*, and all kin[d of] *Flesh-ravishing Melodies*, with filthy *Songs*, and a[b]ominable *Romances*, taught by ingenious Lads [of] *Peccatum's* own Tutoring.

Their Statutes are very easy to the Flesh, bei[ng] wholly under the Law of *Sin*, *Looseness*, and *Sen*[sua]*lity*; and how should it be otherwise, when [Sin] bears the only Rule and Sway; for 'tis he t[hat] reig[ns] reigns in their mortal Bodies, whom they obey in every *Motion* and *Lust* whatsoever.

The Chief Judge that hears and determines all Cases of Doubt and Controversy that may arise, is *Depraved-Judgment*; the other Magistrates are *Wilful Will*, *Deceitful-Memory*, and *Carnal Affections*; the Recorder is, *Mis-led*, *Blind*, and *Evil Conscience*.

As touching the Privileges of the City *Sensuality*, they are very many; tho' I shall mention but Few.

1. The Inhabitants have free Liberty to Trade in any Merchandize the City affords; and learn all the Arts thereof, if they please.

2. To break the *Sabbath-Day*, and play at what *Sports* or *Games* they like best; or carouse it at *Taverns*, *Ale-Houses*, or *Bawdy Houses*.

3. To violate all the good Laws of *God*, *Nature*, and *Nations*.

4. To bring up their Children in the same *Craft*.

5. To reproach and villify all that are *Godly*, *Civil*, or *Honest*.

Lastly, To enter in at the Wide Gate (whenever they die) and go into the Lake that burns with Fire and Brimstone, it being always open for them; but you must know, 'tis he that built this City, and is the chief Governor thereof, who grants all these Privileges; and that is the Devil.

Now, as every City hath a Stock or Treasure belonging to it, so hath this also, *viz*.

1. A Stock of *Infamy*, that can never be exhausted.

2. A Stock of *Filth* and *horrid Pollution*.

3. A Stock of *Guilt*, more than any can stand under.

4. The

98   The Progress of SIN: Or,

4. The Treasure of a *Rotten*, *Diseased*, and *Loathsome Carcass*.

5. A Stock of all the *Threats*, *Plagues*, and *fearful Curses* that are contained in the *Old* and *New Testament*.

Lastly, A whole Heap of *Wrath* treasured up against the Day of Wrath, and Revelation of the righteous Judgments of God.

There is yet one Thing more that I shall note, as touching the Inhabitants of this City, and that is, They are all Soldiers, being trained up from their Childhood in all the Arts of War, to fight under the Banner of the *Prince of Darkness*, against the Great *God* of Heaven and Earth, *Jesus Christ*, and the *Holy Ghost*; whose Motions they are taught continually to resist also, against the *Light of Nature*. And *Lastly*, Against all good *Counsel*, *Reproofs*, or *Exhortations*, that any in Love to their Souls, do at any Time give them.

Yet nevertheless, a poor *Reader* adventured to come to the Gate of the City to say Prayers, and give them good Instructions; and as it appeared, a great Number seemed to attend unto what he said; but some Good-Fellows (who were Students in the Art of *Drunkenness*) observing his Nose, when he had done, enticed him into the City, and got him to a *Tavern*, and made him Beastly *drunk*; which one of the *sensual* Ladies observing, allured him by her bewitching Stratagems to commit *Folly* with her; and I do not hear that he has deserted the City ever since.

But at last, one *Teachgue*, a Godly Divine, was sent by his Blessed Master *Jesus Christ*, to the City-Gate, to Preach the Gospel to them, *Where without, and uttered his Voice in the Streets, in the chief Place of Concourse, in the Opening of the Gates, &c. How long ye simple Ones, will ye love Simplicity, and Scorners delight in Scorning, and Fools hate Knowledge? Turn ye at my Reproof,* Prov. i. 20, 21, 22, 23. Unto you, O Men, I call! Oh! therefore leave your Folly, and forsake your evil Ways; for that God whom you every Day provoke, is like to a consuming Fire, and his Wrath is kindled against you: Therefore, if you do not quit this Place, and fly to the City of Refuge, even now whilst it is called Day, he will bring his Plagues and fearful Judgments upon you.

But if any one of you bless himself in his Heart, saying, *I shall have Peace, tho' I walk in the Imagination of my own Heart, to add Drunkenness to Thirst; the Lord will not spare him; but then the Anger of* Jehovah *shall smoke against that Man, and all the Curses that are written in this Book, shall lie upon him; and the Lord will blot out his Name from under Heaven.*

Oh! you Monsters of Wickedness, will you dare the Almighty? Can you prevail against the Bosses of his Buckler? Can you stand before his Indignation? I am come to call you out of this Hellish City, that is, to leave your Sensual and Beastly Lives, and accept of Pardon through Jesus Christ. Oh! is there none that will lay down their Arms, and close in with the Tenders of Grace: For tho' you are thus wicked, and have done as many evil Things as you could, Jer. iii. 5. yet there is Mercy for you if ye Repent, and Believe in Jesus Christ.

Look about you, for the Lord's Sake! Fire! Fire! Behold the City is on Fire at one End, and also Besieged by the Wrath of God: You are all undone Men and

100   *The Progress of* SIN: *Or,*

Women, if you do not speedily fly out, and save your Lives. You must Turn, or Die. How doth my Soul tremble to behold what is coming upon you! for *A Fire is kindled* (faith God) *in my Anger, which shall burn unto the lowest Hell, and shall consume the Earth, with her Increase, and set on Fire the Foundations of the Mountains,* Deut. xxxii. 22. And he spake to the same Purpose with great Zeal, Courage, and Compassion, Tears standing in his Eyes, beholding their woeful Condition. But most of them did laugh at him, and many abused him with shameful Speeches: Yet some few were wrought upon, and Two or Three more especially drew near to him, bewailing their perishing State; but withal told him, *The City was so strong, they knew not which Way to escape.*

Now, when the rest were gone, he told them, *There was a Little Gate, called* Regeneration; *which, if they could but find, they might get out:* But they said, *It was like that Gate was locked.* Well, said he, tho' it be, yet there is a Key which will open it, and that is, Prayer.

Then they, with many Tears and bitter Sobs, cried to the Lord, and at last they found the *Gate.* But it was a great while before they could find the *Porter,* who is appointed to open the *Gate,* whose Name is *Repentance:* But yet their Eyes being enlightned by the *Spirit of Grace,* they got through the First Wall, which you heard is *Blindness of Mind:* Then they came to the Second Wall, called *Presumption;* and looking about them, they saw divers other poor People just at their Heels, thinking to get away also: But when they beheld this Wall, they all stood still; for between these Two

Gates

Gates lay large *Green Fields*; (these *Green Fields* are the *Pleasures* and *Honours* of the *World*) and those People were resolved to abide there, concluding now they were safe enough; resting wholly upon the *Mercy of God*, and so were kept in the City, under some common *Illuminations* of the *Spirit*, which is the Ruin of many Thousands. For when their *Consciences* are awakened, and they begin to be sensible in some Measure of the woeful State of *Fallen Man*, yet hearing of the infinite Grace and Mercy of *God* in *Christ*, they go no further, but remain in their *Sins*, and never strive after the Gate of *Regeneration*, and yet hope to be saved. But those Three poor Souls before-mentioned, were under a more special and thorough Work: For they called to Mind, how *Theologue* had opened to them the Nature of *God's Justice*, as well as his *Mercy*; and that He would in no wise clear the Guilty; (and that they must therefore utterly forsake *Sin*, *and be born again, or else could not see the Kingdom of* God.) Therefore they durst not presume upon *God's Mercy* whilst they remained in their *Sins*, nor trust to *Latter Repentance*, (which seldom proves true;) by which Means they got through this Wall likewise.

Then they came along with the *Porter* to the Third and Last Wall, called *Unbelief*; which they no sooner beheld, but their Hearts failed them: Wherefore they here stood still, and knew not what to do, fearing *Apollyon* would come out against them, and swallow them up quick (for his Eye was fixed upon them all the while.) And now he bestirred himself to the Purpose, and indeed, threatned them, that if they endeavoured to go further,

he

he would throw them over that Wall into the Moat; out of which few ever escaped with their Lives.

Upon this they trembled: Yet looking back, they saw several Persons were coming up to them, having also got over the Wall of *Presumption*: But lo! on a sudden, they perceived *Apollyon* coming out upon those poor Creatures, and threw One or Two of them into the Ditch, or Moat of *Despair*; and others he forced to retreat back again: But these Three Worthies having heard of the Virtue of *Christ's Blood*, and the Nature of *Gospel Promises*, took fresh Courage; so that the Gate that leads through this Wall, was open also. Yet they had not the Power to venture through: For one of them, more particularly, calling to Mind his notorious, evil and debauched Life, he having lived a long Time in the City of *Sensuality*, perceived the deep and dangerous Moat, (through the Gate) which he concluded he should fall into, and be undone for ever. But the other Two encouraged and strengthened him as much as they could. But alas! all would not do; and indeed, they themselves were full of Fears and Doubtings. But it was not long before a most sweet and lovely *Lady*, with her several *Daughters*, (whom they had met with some Time before, and received Help from) appeared to them, whose Name was *Grace*, who bid them not fear. *For*, said she, *here is my Eldest Daughter*, Faith; *if you can prevail with her, she will soon (with the Aid of my other Daughters) help you all through the Gate of* Unbelief, *and over the Moat of* Despair *too; and indeed, none else can do it.*

But

But *Apollyon* understanding this, immediately most furiously assaulted them; yet *Faith*, by turning her Shield against him, made him quickly fly away; and at last they were resolved to throw themselves upon the *Mercy* of *God*, through the *Blood* of *Jesus Christ*, and adventure over: *And if* (said one to the other) *we perish, we perish; there is nothing but Death if we go back, or remain here.*

And thus they encouraged one another, and ventured in; and *Faith*, that most noble Offspring of God, (with the Help of the other *Graces*) kept them from sinking, so that they all Three escaped. And just as they got over the Moat, they espy'd a clear and lovely Fountain set wide open, *Zech.* xiv. 1. and *Faith* helped them to wash and bathe themselves therein; for they saw they were exceedingly polluted.

After this, they hasted away, as fast as they could go, towards a little Town called *Religion,* (which lies in the direct Way to *New Jerusalem*.) But oh! with what Difficulty did they pass along the Country, for the Enemy pursued them close; so that the first Day they escaped the Moat, they were forced to mount a mighty Hill called *Opposition*. And here they were stopped, not only by *Sin* and *Hellish Temptations*, but the Country People also, were stirred up by the Enemy to turn them back, or hinder them in their Flight. Yet they got up the Mountain; and the next Day they fell down into a deep Valley, called *Self Denial*: So difficult a Passage it is, that but few are able to pass along; and yet there is no other Way to *New Jerusalem*. And presently upon this, they came to a certain Stile, (which they perceived

would.

would also put them hard to it to get over) it being called, The *Stile* of *Carnal-Reason*. Yet they not consulting with *Flesh* and *Blood*, made little of it.

But alas! they were not gone much further, before they came into an *Howling Wilderness*. And here they seemed for a while to be at a Stand, there being so many *Turnings* and *By-ways*: And the Enemy, to amuse them, raised up several subtil *Impostors*, to put them out of the *Right Path*; one crying, *This is the Way*; and another, *That*. Besides, they were assured the *Wilderness* had many *Pits* in it, and it was also very dark and dolesome; so that if they had not met some Time before, with an able and sure *Guide*, doubtless they had perished in this Place. But *Truth* was their *Conductor*; whose Counsel always (as 'tis contained in the *Holy Bible*) they resolved to take, so that they missed not their Way. But it seems, Two or Three Days after, they met with many *Lyons*, and other *evil Beasts*; yet they passed securely along, they having no Power to hurt them; tho' (poor Souls!) they were possessed with great Fear: But *Faith* vanquished their Doubts and Desponding Thoughts.

But yet the worst was not over: For lo! on a sudden they were beset with *Thieves*, who threatned to knock them on the Head, but they were restrained; yet they robbed them of their Cloaths, and Part of their Money. But they, calling to Mind how wonderfully *God* had deliver'd them from *Sin* and *Satan*, matter'd none of all these Things: For now, to their inconceivable Joy and Comfort, they came into the *sweet and pleasant Way of the New Covenant*. And at last, getting up upon the Top of an high Rock, called the *Rock of Ages*, they were

were safe enough; where they had a full View (when they looked downwards) of the miserable Country *Senfuality*, from whence they came; and when they looked upwards, they saw (to the ravishing of their Hearts) the Glory of that *Heavenly Country* they were going to; and where they will arrive in due Time.

But here at present we must leave them, and pursue our History of the Travels of Bloody *Peccatum*.

CHAP. VII.

Shewing how Tyrant Sin came in his Travels into the great Country of Commerce, where formerly stood a Famous Town called Morality; and what fearful Work he made there.

SIN, that cruel Enemy, and Destroyer of Souls, having thus enlarged his Territories, and settled all Things in the Great City *Senfuality*, and left Part of his Retinue and Attendance, with many Infernal Spirits, to watch Night and Day, to keep all in *Carnal Security* there; was resolved (in Company with *Apollyon*) to Travel farther: And in a short Time he came into the Country of *Commerce*, where stood in former Times, that Famous and Honest Town, called *Morality*; which he took up a Resolution to ruin and lay under Ground; or, otherwise, by secret Policy, undo, or utterly beguile or deceive all the Inhabitants. Now, this Town, as I said, hath formerly been in great Esteem,

Esteem, being a Place of good Trade; and many honest and well-meaning People dwelt in it: But this cursed Traveller, it appears, had been in it of Latter Times before now; and by his Subtilty had made it a poor and despised Village, and very thin also of Inhabitants; yet was not satisfied, but designs to raze it, if possible, to the very Foundations thereof.

But since he is got into the Country, and hath also entered the Town, let us observe his present Enterprize.

First, He meets with one Person that is very Rich, and him he intices to augment his Substance; to grind the Face of the Poor, by forcing them to sell their Commodities under the Market Price; (he understanding their Necessities.)

And then he stirred up another, not to lend Money to any, though in never such Distress, without Extortion, or unconscionable Interest; nay, and will have a Pawn, or else not a Penny to be had.

Moreover, Some he enticeth to Monopolize, or engross Commodities so into their own Hands, that none might sell of that, to gain any thing by them but themselves.

Divers others, who for a while seemed sober Persons, and might have lived still in the Town of *Morality*, in good Credit, he allured to Lusts and Wantonness; by which Means he sent them to dwell in the City *Sensuality*.

Likewise, many that were Poor, he teaches to break their Word and Promises; and at last, their Bonds and Covenants, nay, and Oaths too; and never left them, until he, by the Aid of the Devil, had

had made Thieves of them; and sent them to stand upon the Highway.

Also, some he caused in several Kingdoms, to deal unrighteously, and subvert Law and Justice, by which Means sad Havock is made in the Country of *Commerce*, and Town of *Morality*, throughout the World; which caused the Prophet to cry out of Old, *For our Transgressions are multiplied before Thee, and our Sins testify against us: For our Transgressions are with us; and as for our Iniquities, we know them.*

In transgressing and lying against the Lord, and departing away from our God; speaking Oppression and Revolt, conceiving and uttering from the Heart Words of Falshoods.

And Judgment is turned away backward; and Justice standeth afar off: For Truth is fallen in the Streets, and Equity cannot enter.

Yea, Truth faileth, and he that departeth from Evil, maketh himself a Prey: And the Lord saw it, and it displeased Him, that there was no Judgment.

Many he provoketh to borrow Money, and live high, when they know in their Consciences, they are not able to pay it: And after they have run into many Mens Debts, they may make a Break of it, when they have not Five Shillings in the Pound, perhaps, to offer their Creditors.

Some others he causes when far in Debt, to confess Judgments, on purpose to cheat their Neighbours.

And that which is the worst of all, he hath enticed many of latter Times, to shut up their Shops, to make People think they were undone by the Badness of the Times and Trade; and so were

E 6   forced

forced to call their Creditors together, being willing, forsooth, to pay as far as they have; and that not above Eight or Ten Shillings in the Pound, when in Truth, at the same Time, they were worth some Hundreds. Alas! the whole Design was but to cheat others, that they might enrich themselves.

But by this Device many honest People have been undone; and by such too, whom they little suspected would have been led by the Devil to become the worst of Thieves and Robbers: For they out-do those who stand on the Highway; for these more secretly and insensibly rob and undo the People they Trade with. The common Thief Men provide for; being aware of him, they know the better how to secure themselves.

Now, these are some of those Projects Sin plays in these Parts, whereby the Country of *Commerce* is strangely spoiled, there being hardly an honest Man in it: For now-a-days no Man knows who to Trust, nor Trade with.

But, should I open all the Ways, Tricks, and Inventions of *Sin* and *Satan*, by which the Town of *Morality* is invaded, and like utterly to be spoiled, it would fill a great Volume: The Truth is, 'Tis sadly batter'd down, and the Streets are thin of People, as in a Plague-Time. Old Father *Honesty*, and Goodman *Just-Dealing* are both dead; so that if you ask for either of that Name, No-body knows how to direct you. Commodities are prais'd by the Seller, when he knows they are naught; and dis-prais'd by the Buyer, when he sees they are good. Unlawful Profit is took, and yet cries the Shop-keeper, *I cannot afford it cheaper*. And
another

another cries, (nay, and swears too, may be) *He will not abate a Farthing*: And yet, perhaps, rather than lose his Customer, he takes many Pence, if not Shillings less: And all the Time they perceive not the Traveller, nor Satan neither, standing at their Elbow, prompting them thus to do, and laughing to see what a Number of true Slaves and Vassals he has got in this Country; for every one seeks to supplant his Brother.

Now *Sin* having done his worst in this Place, and almost quite ruined the Inhabitants, and left few of the ancient Houses standing (and them so defaced too, that now it may rather be called *Immorality*, than by the Name it was formerly known by) Travelled farther.

CHAP. VIII.

Shewing how Sin, alias Ungodliness, came into the Great City Babylon: and of the Mysterious Exploits and Mischievous Work he made there.

THE Tyrannical Traveller, *Sin*, alias *Ungodliness*, came at last to visit an ancient City, which above Twelve Hundred Years ago he had erected, after a new and mysterious Fashion, in the Confines of the vast Country *Sensuality*, and 'tis called *Great Babylon*.

Indeed it was high Time for him to haste to this City, it being the only Place of Security for him; for there he may have a Pardon (they say) on easy Terms, for all the Villainy that he has done.

But before I proceed to speak of the Trade, Customs, and Privileges of this Great City, it may not be amiss to speak a little concerning the Situation of the Place.

Know then, that the Palace, or chief Seat of the King of *Babylon*, is built upon Seven Hills; where also hath been Seven Sorts of Governments.

Also, by another Mark the City is distinguished from all other Cities in the World, *viz.* 'Tis said to *Reign over the Kings of the Earth.*

'Tis also called, *The Mother-City*, or *Mother-Church*; for you must know, 'tis a Spiritual City.

Moreover, 'tis adorned with all Manner of outward Pomp and Glory, so that there is not the like Splendid Mystical City in the World; and yet it is the City of *Confusion*, (as the Name of it signifies:) And also called, *A Great City*.

'Tis in this City that the *Blood of the* Saints *and* Martyrs *of* Jesus *is found,* (which was in former and latter Times) shed in great Abundance; so that in every Street thereof the Blood doth run down like a great Stream.

As to its Foundation; it is (as they say) built upon St. *Peter*, not upon *Christ*; and yet St. *Paul* saith, *Another Foundation can no Man lay than that which is laid, which is* Jesus Christ, 1 Cor. iii. 11.

But is this City *Babylon* indeed built upon *Peter?* Upon his Person it cannot; that is ridiculous to suppose: Upon his Doctrine, Confession of Christ, and Holy Example it is not; then it must be upon his Defection: You know he denied his Master. O! there the Foundation was laid; for the Truth is, *Apollyon* and *Sin* raised this strange and mysterious Structure in the Ruins of the outward Court of the Holy City, and built it upon *Apostacy, Heresy, Blasphemy, Usurpation, Judaism, Paganism, Imperious Decrees, Decretals, Canons, Ceremonies, Traditions, Superstitions,* and *Unwritten Verities,* or rather very *Lyes.*

Moreover, the Walls of the City are strong, which are these following: 1. *Ignorance.* 2. *Atheism.* 3. *Sensual Pleasures, Honours, Riches.* 4. *Pardons, Absolutions, Indulgence, Inquisition.* 5. *Blood, Massacres, Persecution, Cruelties, Fire* and *Sword,* &c. 6. *Civil, Ecclesiastical,* and *Universal Power,* or pretended *Supremacy* over *Emperors, Kings, Princes, Nobles, Churches,* and all *Nations* and *People* of the *Earth.* 7. *Infalibility.*

'Tis needful also for you to know, That *Sin* hath much Work to do in this Place; for as he (by the subtil and mysterious Working and Aid he had from *Apollyon*) did first erect it; so doth he still uphold, strengthen, and repair it; for it hath in these latter Times gone somewhat to Decay, by Means of the great Wars that have been made against it by the *Lamb* and his Followers.

Now, that which *Sin* by Craft and Subtilty hath done to raise its Fame, and enlarge its Borders, was, partly the great Miracles (it is said) he wrought in the midst of it, to deceive the poor, ignorant, and blind Inhabitants, which indeed were the strangest that ever were heard of in the World.

But that which spoils all, is the Epithet the Holy Apostle gives them, by calling them *Lying Signs and Wonders;* what kind of Miracles they are, you have them recorded in divers Treatises, to which we shall refer you.

But this is not all his Business in this Place; for
he

112 *The Progress of* SIN: *Or,*

he is employed by *Apollyon,* to teach and instruct the People in many strange Articles of Faith, that so he may appear a compleat *Mystery of Iniquity:* Some of which here follow:

1. That the Inhabitants may Swear, Lye, nay, and Forswear themselves (if it be to promote the Good of the *Holy Church*) and yet be *True Men.*

2. They may contrive Rebellions, Murders and Treasons, and yet be *as innocent as the Child unborn.*

3. They may be filled with, and make a Trade of *Excess* and *Drunkenness,* and yet be the Patterns of *Sobriety* and *Temperance.*

4. To commit gross *Idolatry,* and yet be the *True Worshippers* of God.

5. To commit *Fornication* and *Adultery,* and yet be spotless and pure in Heart, and good *Catholicks.*

6. He teaches the King of *Babylon* to elevate himself to the highest Pinacle of Pride, even above Emperors, Kings, and Princes; nay, above *Jesus Christ* and *God* the *Father;* and yet to be so humble, meek, and lowly-minded, as to be content to be called *The Servant* of *Servants.*

7. To slaughter, kill, and barbarously murder Men, Women and Children, that dare not be so Wicked as themselves, and yet be full of Mercy, tender Pity, and Compassion, as an *Apostle, Shepherd, Vicar,* and *Successor* of the Meek and Lamb-like *Jesus.*

8. To cast the Truth to the Ground, deface God's Law, and burn the Holy Bible, and yet be *The True Witnesses* to it, and Maintainers of it.

9. To foment Wars and Broils in most Nations, and contrive the Ruin of many Kingdoms by Fire, Sword, and cruel Devastations, and yet be as *harmless as Doves* to all Mankind.   10. For

The Travels of Ungodliness. 113

10. For a People to be confederate, and join in with, and be guilty of all these unparalell'd Villanies and rapacious Murders, and yet be *The Holy Catholick Church* of God, the *pure and spotless Spouse* of Christ, his *harmless Lambs,* the *only Orthodox Christians,* and *True Followers of the Primitive Saints.*

11. To say, the *Church cannot Err,* tho' God and all the World knows there are not such *Great Errors* in Principles, nor *like Enormities, cursed Actions, cruel* and *immoral Practices* in the World.

12. But the greatest Mystery of all, *Sin* teaches their Priest, *viz.* by a strange Charm of Five *Latin* Words, that is, *Hoc est enim Corpus meum,* (which in *English* is, *For this is my Body*) to Transubstantiate a *Wafer-Cake* into the *Real Body* and *Blood* of Jesus Christ; and this *Breaden-God* the Inhabitants eat, even Flesh, Blood, and Bones, and so (like strange *Cannibal*) devour their *Maker*; and tho' it be utterly against Reason, and contradicted by all the Five Senses, as well as Scripture, yet it must be acknowledged to be nothing else than what we before asserted; and those that will not believe it so to be, and adore it with the highest Degree of Divine Worship, which is proper to God only, must be Anathematized, if not burned at a Stake.

You must know, That here is also a Market kept every Day in the Week, where there are many choice Commodities sold.

The Merchandize of this City are very rich, as you have them laid down in the Holy Scripture, *viz. The Merchandize of Gold and Silver, Precious Stones, Pearls, Fine Linnen, Purple, Silk, Scarlet, and all sweet Wood, with all manner of Vessels of Ivory, and all manner of Vessels of precious Wood,*

and

and of *Brass*, *Iron* and *Marble*, and *Cinnamon*, *Odours*, *Ointments*, *Frankincense*, *Wine*, fine *Flour*, *Wheat*, *Beasts*, *Sheep*, *Horses*, *Chariots*, *Slaves*, and *Souls of Men*, &c. Rev. xviii.

If you do but observe the last Commodity, you cannot but say they Trade in Things of great Worth; for what is more precious than the Souls of Men?

Also here is to be had that Staple Commodity of the whole City of *Babylon*, viz. *Pardons* and *Indulgencies* of all Sorts and Sizes, for all and all Manner of Sins, of whatsoever Shape or Complexion they be (on easy Terms) whether past, present, or to come; also a certain Release for Souls that have lain long in the searching Flames of *Purgatory*.

Moreover, at this Fair or Market are rare Shows or Sights to be seen; yea, such Rarities that the World cannot afford the like, viz. Part of the *Cross* on which our Saviour was Crucified; the *Tail* of the *Ass* on which he rode to *Jerusalem*; great Store of the Virgin *Mary's Milk*; also the *Thread*, *Work-Basket*, *Scissars*, and *Needles* which were used in making Christ's Seamless-Coat, &c.

If Rome *can pardon Sins, as* Romans *hold;*
And if those Pardons can be Bought and Sold,
Were it a Sin to adore and worship Gold?
If they can purchase Pardons with a Sum,
For Sins they may commit in Time to come,
And for Sins past, who would not haste to Rome?
But oh! the plaguy Thing of being poor!
For is it not a lamentable Story,
For want of Gold, to lie for evermore
In Hell, or at the least in Purgatory?

Out

*Out of which Place can never come the Poor,
No, nor the Rich, without they'll waste their Store.*

Lastly, The Enemy teaches the Inhabitants of Great City the rare Art and Mystery of *Equitation,* by which he is had in great Veneration one'st them.

Besides, he is, you must know, a rare Politician, being the chief Agent to carry on, and contrive all the dark and bloody Intrigues of State amongst them.

But since I hear he is very busy to stir up, and push on another great War against the *Holy Seed,* and *City of God,* we will at present say no more of his Wonders and strange Projects here; but follow him in his Travels, in carrying on of his next Grand Enterprize.

But to the Hearts of such who love *Zion,* this let me note by the Way; that is, 'Tis not doubted by most of the *Faithful,* but that the *Fall* and utter *Overthrow* of this Great *Babylon* is at Hand, and then shall *Zion* be delivered. *And the same Hour there was a great Earthquake, and the tenth Part of the City fell,* Rev. xi. 13. *When she saith in her Heart, I sit a Queen, and shall see no Sorrow, nor have Loss of Children any more; then in an Hour shall her Judgments come upon her.*

CHAP.

CHAP. IX.

Shewing how Peccatum, *alias* Ungodliness *came against the Town of* Religion (*otherwise called* Sion, *or the City of God*) *with a great Army of a mixt People, and Besieged it: Moreover, how he met with* True Godliness, *and a Noble Citizen of* Mount Zion, *called* Thoughtful; *and what Discourse past betwixt them: With the Strange, Politick, and Bloody Stratagems the Tyrant used to destroy the Holy City: Together with a compendious Description of the Situation, Foundation, Trade, and Privileges thereof; and by what Means it holds out against all the Powers of Darkness.*

U*Ngodliness* having not yet done his Travels, though he had settled Matters pretty well in Great *Babylon*, ranges about, and destroys wonderfully in every Kingdom and Nation; neither doth he spare any, where, either by Force or Fraud, he can prevail; pitying no Sex nor Degree of People, High nor Low, Noble nor Ignoble, Rich nor Poor, Old nor Young; for such is his Impudence, that he assaults the Prince upon the Throne, as well as the Beggar on the Dunghil, insomuch that he (as it is said) hath got strange Footing or Entertainment in the Courts of Emperors, Kings, and many other Mighty Ones o the Earth, alluring them by his Policy, to take Arms for him: And having by this Means gathered together a vast and prodigious Army, resolved to enter upon his last grand and main enterprize, which was, to Besiege, Attack, and lay desolate the *Holy City*; which, by gracious Providence, hath in these latter Times been rebuilt. And now you must know, that this Army doth consist of, or is made up with People of divers Nations; as, *Turks, Tartars, Mahometans, Babylonians, Atheists,* and a Multitude besides, brought out of the great Country and City *Sensuality*, with another Sort of dangerous Enemies; which we shall speak more hereafter.

Never was *Sin* and *Ungodliness* raised up to higher Pomp and Grandeur than he seems at this Time; for lo! now he is mounted on Horseback, as a glorious Conqueror, leading the numerous Hosts, like a victorious General, or Commander in Chief under *Apollyon,* King of the *Bottomless-Pit*; having Thousands of Thousands following him, with great Shouts, Musick of all Sorts, and loud Acclamations; crying, *Great is Diana of the whole World.*

As touching the Martial or Warlike Order they march in against Mount *Sion*; take this briefly:

Peccatum leads the Van (being himself more than a Hundred Thousand strong.)

Next to him marches *Apollyon,* mighty *Beelzebub,* and *Lucifer,* heading three great Armies, composed of different kinds; yet all cruel Enemies to this City.

The First consisteth of the *Riches* of this *World*; by which Thousands have fallen.

The Second of *Honours* and *sinful Preferments.*

The

The Third is filled up with *Vain Delights* and *Pleasures.*

They are also called by Three other Names, viz. *The Lust of the Eyes, the Lust of the Flesh,* and *the Pride of Life.*

After these, a Man adorned in *Cloth of Gold* with a *Triple Crown* on his Head, and for a *Scepter* a Brace of *Keys* in his Hand, who I take to be the Great King of *Babylon,* with a glorious Retinue of *Cardinals, Patriarchs, Bishops, Abbots, Friars, Monks, Nuns, Seminaries, Jesuits,* and Number more following him, with a great Train of Artillery; as, *Merit of Works, Limbus, Purgatory, Pardons, Indulgencies, Vows, Prayers to* and *for the Dead, Penance, Holy Water, Pilgrims, Auricular Confession, Extream Unction, Lamps, Candles, Torches, Tapers, Relicks, Oil, Salt, Spittle, Crucifixes, Beads, Holy Garments, Signs, Gestures, Canons, Customs,* and what not besides; as, *Bloody Slaughters, Massacres, Stakes, Fire* and *Sword.*

Then comes the *Grand Signior,* or the proud and blasphemous Emperor of *Turky,* attended with his chief *Mufti,* and a Multitude of other inferior Priests, with their *Alcoran* in their Hands, and a great Army at their Heels, with Swords, and other slaughtering Weapons, swearing by their *Bear* what they will do to such as oppose them; being all true Sons and Vassals to *Apollyon,* and the dreadful Enemy, *Peccatum.*

And then after these, an Army of *fair Ladies* dress'd up in sumptuous Apparel, and in the new Mode the City *Sensuality* hath of late found out; as, *spotted Faces, naked Breasts* and *Shoulders.*

And with them a Number of *debauched Lads,*

of *Youth-shire*, armed *Cap-a-pee*; being as true as Steel to the Interest of their beloved Leader, and very expert in all Stratagems of War against *God, Christ*, and *True Godliness*.

Moreover, besides these, a bloody and treacherous Brigade, who lie in secret Ambuscade, who are as dangerous as any of the rest, called *In bred Corruption*.

In the Rear marches Two Regiments: The First being made up of a base Sort of Varlets, called *Renegades*, that is, being such who have deserted the Lord *Jesus Christ*, and the *Holy City*, and joined in with the Enemy, who are become as cruel Adversaries as any in the World.

The last was a Regiment of strange People, hardly Two of them being alike, and their Manners and Customs were as various: They came out of a Town which lies on one Side of the *City of God*, called *Heresy*; being rotten at Heart, and corrupt in the Fundamentals of the *True Christian Religion*; holding almost every abominable *Principle* that hath been broached by the Devil in any Age of the Church.

This War being proclaimed, and all the Forces of Hell and Darkness mustered, a Council was called to consult about the best Expedients to carry it on: And there being neither Power nor Policy wanting, what can we think should be the Issue of it, but Ruin and Slaughter to the *Holy Seed*.

Now the great Design on Foot, 'tis thought is, how to kill the *Witnesses*: But *Apollyon* judged it at this Juncture, to send *Peccatum*, as a subtil Spy into the City first, to see if he could by Treachery get the Gates open to his Armies.

The Instructions he received, were as follows:

Apollyon. DEAR *Peccatum,* though our Armies are ready, and all Things promise fair, yet great Part of the Work will lie upon Thee and I: And indeed thou must now bestir thee; for the Inhabitants of this City are many of them expert in War, and are not ignorant of our Devices; therefore this must be done:

First, Let us chuse advantageous Seasons to assault them.

Secondly, Manage our Arms in such Methods as best suit with our Craft and Policy.

Thirdly, Pitch on fit Instruments to carry on our Design.

1. As to proper and advantageous Seasons, that is that which gives Facility and speedy Dispatch to a Business. I have often took Men here, because *they knew not their Time:* A small Strength will do at one Time, that a far greater cannot at another.

1. Therefore, when they are newly wrought upon by the *Grace of God,* or a new *Convert* is made, then bestir thyself; for indeed the Cry of the *New Creatures* gives whole Legions of us Devils an Alarm: Alas! their Strength then is weak; see if you can lead them into *Error,* or puff them up with *Pride,* or drive them into *Despair,* by laying before them their former evil Lives.

2. When we see any attended with great Afflictions: This is like a blind solitary Lane, where we as Thieves, may easily beset them; and when they are robbed of all their worldly Comforts, let's tempt them to Impatience, and to conclude God hath forsaken them, and then their Business is done.

When

122 *The* Progress *of* SIN: Or,

When the City wants Provision, or is greatly straightned, then let us sound a Parley.

3. When they are about some notable Enterprize for God's Glory, then thou must be as an *Adder in the Path, that biteth the Horse's Heels, so that the Rider shall fall backwards.* Thus I hindered *Joshua*, by holding his Right-hand, which is the working Hand: We must prevent that Enterprize, by raising up some Difficulty or another.

4. When they are in the Presence of some fit Object to enforce our Temptation, that's our Time: Thus I caught *Eve*, when she was near the Tree, and had the Fruit thereof before her Eyes.

5. When they are asleep, idle, or off their Watch, doubt not but this Way we may surprize the City, and their Souls too with much Ease; for thus Thou and I overcame *David* and the *foolish Virgins*, &c.

6. We must beset them after great Manifestations of God's Love to them; for they shall neither be able to bear well his Frowns nor his Smiles, if we can help it; for we may make the one like to warm Gleams, to bring up the Weeds of Corruption and the other like sharp Frost, to nip and kill the Bud of their Hopes, Grace and great Expectation.

7. Let us come upon them when they seem secure, flourishing in the midst of Peace, Plenty and Prosperity; for that Way we destroyed the Children of *Israel*, when they came into the Land of *Canaan*, and Thousands more in every Nation.

8. 'Tis good to assault them before they have learned the crafty Use of their Arms; for an unexperienced Soldier is soon brought under.

9. We must be sure to come upon them in the Night of God's Withdrawings: When their G

neral is absent, let us be present; when he hides his Face, we will soon shew our Heads.

10. *Lastly*, At their *Dying Hour*; for if we cannot do our Work before, let us strive to do it then; for this is the last Cast for the Game: Now, or Never.

II. We must use our utmost Craft in managing our Assaults. Therefore,

1. Let us find out their Natural Inclinations and Dispositions; there's one Sin or another that easily besets them; where the Walls of the City are weakest we must raise our Batteries: Thou mayest get in at one Place, when thou canst not at another. I need say no more; observe this well.

2. As need shall require, hang out false Colours, and pretend to be as much for *real Sanctity* as the best of them; but when all is done, cause them to rely upon it; for this Way they'll become over-righteous, and so destroy themselves.

3. We must continually get Intelligence of their Affairs: Let our Eyes be upon them at Home or Abroad, so that nothing may be wanting on our Parts on any Occasion, to help on their *Commission of Evil*, or *Omission of Good*: That which seems a *Mole-hill* in the Way of their Duty, let us make a *Mountain*; if we can keep them from their *Temple*, we may soon bring them to our *Synagogue*.

4. Let us make our Approaches gradually: We must not ask too much at first; a few may be let into the City, when a great Army cannot: Thou mayest persuade them to go a Mile or two, tho' not to the End of thy Journey; shew them first the Object, and afterwards tempt them to Desire; thou may'st get in thy Foot, where thou canst not get in thy Head.

5. We

5. We must (if possible) Unarm them; however, take away their Sword, tho' we cannot their Shield, that they may not wound our Friends, tho' we cannot slay them. Our *Babylonian* Army are excellent Artists at this Sort of Fighting; if they can but enter the City, they'll soon rid their Hands of this Weapon, so that they shall never cut their Fingers more with it; in the mean Time, we must render it insufficient, or blunt the Edge as much as may be, and magnify the Light within, or *Unwritten Traditions* about it, that it may do the le[ss] Mischief.

6. Let us sometimes retreat in Policy, when w[e] are in a fair Way to get the Victory. We *Unclea[n] Spirits* sometimes seem to go out of Men, wh[en] our Design is to return seven times stronger tha[n] before: If thou canst but persuade them to lo[ve] thee, I am content they should in part leave thee for I had rather see thee in their Affections, tha[n] in their Conversations.

7. We must never raise our present Siege, ti[ll] we have starved them: No better Way in th[e] World to deal with these Enemies, than to cut o[ff] Provisions, and other Recruits from coming to them

8. Let us destroy (if possible) their bold Leader[s] (who so oft sally out of the City upon us) and ei[-] ther by Force or Flattery bring them to lay dow[n] their Arms, and then the rest will be afraid: Whe[n] the Pillars fall, the House will follow.

9. 'Tis one great Part of thy Work to end[ea-] vour to break their Ranks, and put them into [dis-] order; for then thou wilt with Ease conquer.

10. Also cause some of them to lag behind [and] straggle from their Colours, and not regard

Sound of the Trumpet, neither Call nor Alarm; for such will quickly become a Prey to us.

11. But above all Things (if possible) spoil that plaguy Engine that mauls us so fearfully, (I mean *Prayer* and *Fasting*.) Let us do what we can to make that of little Use, or keep them ignorant of the damnable Hurt it hath done us; or blind their Eyes, that they may not know how to mount it upon the Wheels of Faith; or else quench the Spirit which should give Fire to it.

12. Do also what thou canst to force them to Mutiny; if we can divide them, we shall soon devour them; and indeed we have pretty well herein succeeded already.

III. We must make use of fit Instruments to carry on our Designs against them.

1. We must employ Men of Parts and Policy, who have Depth of Reason to argue them out of their Religion. A bad Cause needs a smooth Orator. *Alexander* the *Copper-Smith* (of Old) did me much Good; I matter not what Harm *Paul* sustaineth.

2. Let us set on some Grave, Wise, and Old Apostates to attack them; for hardly better Champions, nor truer Drudges, have we to do this Service for us in all our Armies.

3. We must look out some rare Wits that are well skilled in the Art of Slandering, to load them with Reproach and Infamy, to render them odious to the Vulgar, and thereby hinder others from siding with them: We have whole Regiments of these Boys at hand.

4. Make use of a Husband, a Wife, a Landlord, or such like Persons, to allure them to our Party;

Party; for they (doubtless) will have the greatest Influence upon them.

The Hellish Lecture being ended, the Tyrant hasted towards the City; but lo! before he came very near, he chanced to hear one cry, *Which is the Way?* and another, *Oh! how may I find the City of God!*

At last this cursed Traveller told them he could direct them: For (said he) *I have often been at this City, and know the Way very well.* But instead of directing them into the right Way, he set them in a broad Road, which at last brought them into the Great City *Babylon*: Some others also he put into By-paths, that led them into that pernicious and blasphemous Town, called *Error* and *Heresy*; and there those poor deluded Souls have lived ever since, and take that Place to be the *Holy City*: But at last up comes one boldly, who seemed to have the perfect Knowledge of the Way; and the cruel Enemy seeing him, endeavoured to turn him back, by laying many sad Discouragements before him: But *Apollyon* presently whisper'd the Tyrant in the Ear to let him alone; I know, said he, this Person well enough, he will do our Interest no Harm by entering in; he is a Spy that I have sent to betray the Place.

After him came another; but *Apollyon* cried Let him go into the Town also; for I perceive he bears the World on his Back, and hath a secret Love and Liking to thee too; 'tis only a troublesome Fellow (one *Conscience*) that hath scar'd him to fly from the *Wrath to come*; or else the Fellow would have a Name, &c. 'Tis somewhat of his Nature that causes him to seek a Dwelling here for his Will and Affections stand true and firm to us: And let me tell thee, he will e'er long haste as fast out of this City, as now he seems to hasten into it; and then we shall gain by this Means exceedingly.

1. For, if he deserts *Religion*, and lies out of the *City of God*, he will rejoice all our good Friends, and open their Mouths wide against all the Inhabitants of this Place: For we will make them conclude, and swear too, that all the rest are like him, *viz.* carnal and covetous Persons, and such who love the World above *Christ*.

2. If he returns back into the City *Sensuality*, he will thereby declare, that the Pleasures, Honours and Riches of this World are better Things, and rather to be chosen, than whatsoever he could find in the *City of God*; or if he goes into the City *Babylon*, it will be of like Importance to us, and as much for our Advantage every Way.

3. Moreover, by this Act of his, we shall stumble divers Souls who have Thoughts to go thither, and utterly stifle their Convictions in respect of Duty and Obedience to the Laws and Statutes of that Place.

4. It will wound and grieve the Hearts of our Enemies (the Inhabitants I mean of Mount *Zion*.)

5. It will also weaken their Hands too, and so make the Place the more easy to be taken; for there are (I must tell thee) Multitudes of this Sort got in amongst them, that I shall make the City too hot for, e'er I have done.

6. This will cause *Religion* also itself to become very contemptible.

7. Hereby he will dishonour God, and cause him to cast him off for ever.   8. And

8. And so we shall devour him, and all such at our Pleasure.

9. Also, hereby he will wound his own Soul, and be set in the ready Road to *sin the unpardonable Sin*, which we cannot cause every one to commit.

10. *Lastly*, It will also greatly rejoice all us Devils; for we love to see Mankind guilty of our Sin, which was *Apostacy*, and so fall under our *Condemnation*; and indeed, there is nothing like this makes them more conformable to our Image. At the hearing of these Things, the treacherous Monster lets the Man go in quietly.

But behold, on a sudden, came another who had an honest Heart, whose Name was *Neophitus*, (a Young Christian.) But O how did he bestir himself to block up his Way; so that he was in amaze and greatly feared he should never find the City. But whilst he was looking this Way and that Way, seeing many Cross-turnings, he saw two or three Men coming towards him; now, who should they be, but *True Godliness*, *Theologus*, with the most Noble and Renowned *Thoughtful*; who were come, it seems, to direct poor Strangers the ready Way to the *City of God*. Now *Godliness* perceiving the poor young Christian amazed, asked him what he ailed: *Ah! Sir*, said he, *I would fain go to Mount Zion, that Holy City; and here is a Traveller that has so confounded me, that I cannot find the Way to it*. With that, the Heavenly Prince being full of Holy Zeal, cast an angry Look upon the Enemy and spoke to this Purpose: *O full of all Subtilty and all Mischief, thou Child of the Devil; thou Enemy of all Righteousness; wilt thou not cease to pervert the right Ways of God? I have heard of*

The Travels of Ungodliness.   129

you in my Travels; and have I now met with you? I shall tell you News will make you tremble before I leave you.

Ungodliness. Sir, you seem very hot, and have not lost your Spirit I perceive, tho' you have met with no better Entertainment Abroad where you have been.

Godliness. I thought how you would insult over me; you shew from whence you proceed: Sir, it has been thro' your deluding and ensnaring Wiles, that I have been so slighted: You, and your Hellish Master have put me into such a Disguise, that most of the Inhabitants of the Earth do not know me; besides, you have put out all their Eyes, and filled their Hearts with bitter Enmity against me; but do not suppose I am therefore discouraged, or think the worse of myself; for I have met with as good Usage as my Master *Christ* did, when he lived here on the Earth. I do not doubt but you have met with Entertainments to your Master's Content.

Ungodli. Truth Friend, thou sayest right, all the World is in Love with me, and their Doors are wide open to me where-ever I come; and doth this grieve you?

Godli. It would be strange should I rebuke you for Swearing and Vain glorying; but do not wonder if I am troubled to hear of your great Success in your Soul-undoing Travels.

Ungodli. You want a Cordial; the News I tell you makes you sick: But why should not I be as true to the Interest of my great Master, as you are to yours? Sir, I can't do otherwise.

Godli. I know indeed, your Nature is such, that if you should cease serving *Apollyon*, your Hellish

F 5   Prince

Prince and Sovereign, you would lose your very Being: But this will not serve your Turn.

Ungodli. I know not what you mean; but if you please, let us discourse a little about our Travels: What's the Reason I am so generally embraced, and You slighted?

Godli. I have given you two Reasons of it already; and for the Sake of this poor Young Christian that is by, I will discover other Causes and Grounds of it.

First, 'Tis because you seek in all your Travels, how to please and gratify the Flesh; and I contrariwise teach them to crucify the Flesh, and keep it under, and make no Provision for it, to fulfil the Lusts thereof.

2. You teach Men to mind the Good only of their Bodies, and never regard their Souls: But I tell them they must prefer the Good and Well-being of their Souls a Thousand Times above any thing they judge may be for the Delight or Profit of the Outward Man; because 'tis worth more than all the World.

3. 'Tis because you, by the Help of your Master, and their own deceitful Hearts, have made Brutes of Millions of them; as if they were created for no other End than to please their sensual Appetites.

4. 'Tis because the Presents you offer to them, agree and suit so well with their evil and depraved Natures, which can only savour such Things; but my Dainties none can relish, but by *Faith,* which only belongs to the *New Creature.*

5. 'Tis because your Things are present Things, to be had and enjoyed now; but the best Things

that

that I offer them, are not to be had hereafter.

6. In a Word, 'Tis because you have so hardned their Hearts, and blinded their Minds, by appearing to them in a Disguise, that they (poor Creatures) generally take you to be a Friend, tho' the worst Enemy to them under the Heavens, designing nothing less, than to destroy and damn their Souls for ever.

7. *Lastly*, 'Tis because my Blessed Sovereign, hath for Reasons best known to himself, finding them so evil, hid the Things of which I speak, from the greatest Part of Mankind, and only revealed them to a few.

Ungodli. I am glad you have no more to say, you Enemy of Hell; I see how odious you render me. What I have done, I will still do, and under the same Disguise I have appeared, I will appear; and I have put you into a Disguise too, and could tell you, Fool, that this is one Reason you are entertained by no more. I have put you into a seditious, factious, ignominious, contemptible, and melancholy one; and in it I will keep you, in spite of your Teeth, do your worst, Sir; I regard you not, since I am beloved by Emperors and mighty Potentates of the Earth: I shall never be without Credit; and whilst I have so many Wise and Learned Ones to plead for me and take my Part, I warrant you I shall make your Company thin enough; if that won't do, you know I have another Way to deal with your Favourites; my slaughtering Boys and Weapons are ready for them; and tho' you think you are like to get this Youngster out of my Clutches, you will find yourself mistaken; for I, in the Face of you and your two Champions, will shew you some of my Skill.

Godli. Silence your blasphemous Tongue, I will try a Bout with you; and it shall cost me my Life, and the Life of my two Servants, but we will safely conduct this honest Soul to the *City of God.*

Ungodli. Hey Boys, up go We! By mighty *Belzebub*, I'll to't then: Come, doubtful Soul, be wise, and venture no farther; don't you see how many Cross-ways and Turnings there be?

Neop. I am at a Loss indeed; but I hate you, for what I have heard from you now.

Godli. Child, here is a Blessed Directory for thee, that shews the Way plainly; (with that he put a *Bible* into his Hand) and *Theologue* open'd the Meaning, and gave him the true Sense of it, so that he plainly saw, that the Way, more generally, was *Christ* himself as a Mediator. 1. As a *Priest*, to die for him, to appease the Wrath of God, and satisfy Justice. 2. As a *King*, to subdue this Tyrant *Sin*, and to rule in him, and reign over him, according to those holy and wholesome Laws and Ordinances contained in that Book (which he held in his Hand.) 3. As a *Prophet*, to teach and instruct him. 4. As a *Holy Example* or *Pattern* to imitate and follow. But more particularly, he saw the Way into the City was by *Repentance*, *Faith*, and *Obedience*; then he rejoiced, and praised God.

Ungodli. Do you rejoice, Friend? I will assure you, your Danger is great, if you go further; for there are mighty Armies coming against this City.

Godli. Do not regard him in this Thing. *Who can harm thee, if thou be a Follower of that which is good?* They can't take away thy *God*, thy *Christ*, nor thy Peace from thee. Moreover, the same Troubles and Dangers attended those Saints who are now shining and triumphing in Heaven, and that Power that helped them, is engaged for thee: Besides, thy Troubles and Dangers here are but for a Moment, and they will soon be over; but if thou wilt seek to save thy Life, and escape Trouble, thou wilt lose thy Life, and be exposed to Eternal Death and Danger in Hell: Besides thy Profit will be more than thy Loss; for *Godliness with Contentment is great Gain*: Nay, and let me tell thee, The City has been besieged near these Six Thousand Years, and yet it holds out still: Do not fear, for God hath promised to be a *Wall of Fire round about it*, Zech. ii. 5.

Neop. Come, Sir, let's go.

Ungodli. Go! You are not mad, are you? Some Thousands of People have deserted the City; and is this a Time to go thither?

Godli. It was so, because they were never quite out of Love with this vile Enemy, nor thoroughly converted: But hark! because *Demas* leaves this City, must St. *Paul* do so too? Or because many forsook *Christ*, and walked no more with him, shall his Holy Apostles forsake him? Or, Because the greatest Part of the World go in at the Broad Gate, wilt thou not go in at the Straight?

Neop. God forbid, Sir; this Traveller is, I see, a Deceiver.

Ungodli. Don't abuse me, I am thy Friend, and would have thee pity thyself; for this City no Man regardeth.

Godli. You are his Enemy, and a Murderer: Poor Soul! this is the same that was said of *Zion* of Old Time. *Ungodli.*

Ungodli. The Laws and Ordinances, Friend, are very hard and difficult to keep.

Godli. They are hard indeed to the Flesh, yet to the Spirit very sweet and easy, and not grievous; as the Apostle testifies; nor to the Flesh so hard neither, as was the Service and Work Jesus Christ performed for thy Sake; besides, set the Necessity of doing thy Duty against the Difficulty that attends thee in it; for the Honour of God, and the bearing up his Name in the World is concern'd in it, together with the Increase and strengthening of thy Graces, with the blessed Peace and Comfort of thy precious Soul; for the *Lord meeteth him that rejoiceth and worketh Righteousness, and that remembers him in his Ways,* Isa. lxiv. 5. Besides, consider the Recompence that attends this difficult Work: *Moreover, by them is thy Servant warned, and in keeping of them there is great Reward.*

Ungodli. There is Salvation to be had, Sir, without the Walls of this City.

Godli. There is no Promise of Salvation made to those who sin against their Light, and willingly refuse to follow Christ: The Promise runs to the obedient Soul, to them that obey him, to them that keep his Commandments; besides, without it they are *Dogs, Sorcerers, Whoremongers, Murderers, and whosoever loveth and maketh a Lie,* Rev. 22. 15.

Ungodli. Come, say what you will, they are poor, mean, and despicable People who are within the City: How many Noble, Wise, and Mighty Men after the Flesh, have their Habitations there?

Godli. Thus the *Jews* said of Old, *Have any of the Rulers, or the Pharisees believed on him? But this People who know not the Law, are cursed,* John vii. 47, 48, 49.

Tho'

Tho' they are outwardly Poor many of them, yet they are inwardly Rich; Poor in Temporals, but Rich in Spirituals: But hark! *Hath not God chosen the Poor of this World Rich in Faith, Heirs of the Kingdom, which he hath promised to them that love him?* James ii. 5. Besides, there are some Rich and Honourable, and have been in all Ages, who dwell in this City: St. *Paul* doth not say, *Many Mighty or Noble are called*, tho' he says, *Not many*, &c 1 *Cor.* i. 26.

Ungodli. The greatest Part of the World value other Cities far above it.

Godli. The whole World is said to lie in Wickedness, and the greatest Part of it are deceived by this cunning Impostor; and hence it is they love Darkness rather than Light. *The Way is narrow, and the Gate straight that leadeth unto Life, and few there be that find it.*

Ungodli. Alas! the Inhabitants are at Variance, the City is divided, and they love not one another.

Godli. I must confess, now thou hast hit it; this is too true, but what then? Was the True Church without Divisions? Was it not so with the *Corinthians?*

Ungodli. Say what you please, they are all but a Company of *Schismaticks*, and vile *Hereticks*.

Godli. Soul, regard him not; the *Papists* always after this Manner charged the Saints and Servants of God, because they left their polluted Synagogue. 'Tis one Thing to be accused thus, for leaving the True Religion and Church of God; and another Thing to bear this Brand for forsaking and separating from a false Faith and Church; for so all True Protestants ever affirmed and maintained the

Church

Church of *Rome* to be. *After that Way you call Heresy, so I teach Men to worship the God of their Fathers*, &c.

Ungod'l. Come, come, Friend, if you will be so venturous to go to this City, you will not be able to abide there long; and if you be subject to Gospel Ordinances, and become a Citizen of *Zion*, and afterwards fall away, and desert the Place, your State will be sad; for then you will not only bring up an evil Report upon the City, but also must perish for ever; for there will remain for you no more Sacrifices for Sin.

Godli. Let not this frighten thee, poor Soul; for God hath promised to put his Fear so into thy Heart, that thou shalt not depart from him: His Covenant is an Everlasting One, ordered in all Things, and sure, and whom he loves, he loves to the End. The very same, *Whom he calls, he also justifies, and them whom he justifies, them he also glorifies.* Christ gives to all his Sheep Eternal Life, and none of them shall perish, nor can any pluck them out of his Hand.

Ungod'l. Friend, You are a vile Sinner, and not worthy to have a Dwelling in the *City of God*; for the Truth is, 'Tis a lovely Place, and too good and honourable for such as you are.

Godli. What a Serpent is here! One while 'tis a bad City, and not worth Regard, and what not; and now 'tis so good, he would persuade thee thou art not worthy to have a Dwelling in it. Suppose it should be so, wilt thou therefore refuse to go thither? Art thou worthy of the Bread thou eatest, or of the Drink thou drinkest, or of the Cloaths thou wearest? Why, yet thou dost not refuse these Things because of thy own Unworthiness; even

so

so do not hearken to this cursed Impostor, and refuse Christ's Merits and Ordinances, and a Place in this Blessed City, because not worthy of any of them; the more unworthy thou seest thyself to be, the more welcome thou art there: Come along with us.

Ungodli. If thou steppest one Step further, I'll raise all the Forces of Hell upon thee; my Armies are approaching to my Assistance; therefore I conjure you in the Name of *Apollyon* and *Belzebub*, and all the Powers of the *Infernal Lake*, to desist your Purpose. What say'st thou, wilt thou submit thyself to my Mercy, and be subject to my Authority?

Neop. Blessed be God, I fear thee not, I have found out this Day mine Enemy: Thou Child of the Devil, do'st begin to threaten me? I yield myself conquer'd, but not by the Force of thy Army. Come, Holy Prince and Brethren, let us go to Mount *Zion*, 'tis the City of my Father, of whom glorious Things are spoken. O how I long to be there! Pray let us be gone. Then they all Four fell a singing of Psalms of Praise and Thanksgiving to God; which the grim Monster perceiving, began to foam and rage fearfully, and *Apollyon* grinn'd his Teeth to see the Combat end thus to his Loss, and also cast a most terrible Look upon poor *Thoughtful*, and could hardly forbear to revenge himself by falling upon him, but that he saw he was compleatly armed from Head to Foot, with his Sword drawn in one Hand, and his Shield in the other, having all his Glorious Retinue with him. The Tyrant hereupon began to slink away, 't before he went, swore He would e'er long blow
up

up the whole City at once with Gun-powder; but *True Godliness* seeing what a Rage he was in, called to him, and told him, he had sad News to acquaint him with.

Ungodli. What is that?

Godli. What? For certain there is a Warrant signed and sealed, and already gone out against you, to Apprehend you, and bring you to the Judgment-Seat.

Ungodli. Who shall Try me?

Godli. You shall hear that e'er long.

Ungodli. A pretty Story!

Immediately all the Powers of Hell vanished in great Disorder, the Tyrant being somewhat startled at the News he heard; and the Three Noble Worthies, with the Heavenly Prince (*True Godliness*) went on with much Joy, and got all safe into the Holy and Beloved City; of which in the next Place I shall give you a brief Description.

CHAP. X.

A compendious Description of Mount Zion, the City of God, that is Besieged by the Powers of Darkness; together with the Reasons why it holds out still.

FIRST, As to its Situation, 'tis very Beautiful, being built upon that firm and everlasting Rock, *Jesus Christ*.

As to the Laws and Statutes of it, they are all contained in *Christ's New Testament*; the Holy Scripture being the Great *Magna Charta* of the Church.

As touching the Government of it, the Lord *Jesus* is the Chief or Supream Ruler, Judge, and Law-giver of this Spiritual Corporation; and under him are Bishops and Deacons, &c. who are appointed by him to administer Justice and Righteousness to all its Inhabitants.

The Trade or Merchandize of it, *is better than the Merchandize of Gold*, &c. They all deal in one and the same Commodities, *fetching their Riches from afar*, where their Blessed Correspondent *Jesus Christ* is, and makes them glorious and quick Returns. They deal not in any prohibited, counterfeit, nor corruptible Goods.

As to the Nature of this City's Commodities, they are of a Soul-enriching Nature, their Worth not to be valued enough.

1. The *Truth*, which is the first is offered to sale whilst the Market lasteth; which there is fear will end e'er long. *Buy the Truth therefore, and sell it not.*

2. The Second Commodity is, *The Gifts and Graces of the Spirit.*

3. *The Pearl of great Price*, worth Ten Thousand Worlds.

4. Now, as the Trade and Commerce of this City lies principally in *Merchandize fetched from far*, so there is also a glorious River which runs through every Street, which is Navigable, by means of which all those glorious Commodities are conveyed to it, whereby the City is wonderfully enriched. Now this River proceeds from the *Throne of God and the Lamb*, and is as clear as Chrystal; the Nature also of the Water of this River is admirable.

As

240 *The Progress of* SIN: Or,

As touching the Privileges, Franchises, and Immunities of this Spiritual City, as they are great so are they good.

1. *Freedom from Sin*; that is, from the Guilt, Filth, Power, and Punishment thereof, which comprehends Pardon of all Iniquity. This Freedom cost dear; no less than the Price of Christ's most precious Blood. Also, 'Tis a Sealed Freedom, Sealed by the Holy Spirit. *Thirdly,* 'Tis a lasting Freedom, never to be revoked by the Giver, nor forfeited by the Receiver; *I will remember their Sins no more.* 2. *Privilege,* that is, Union with God. 3. *Justification.* 4. *Sanctification.* 5. *Adoption.* 6. *Acceptation.* 7. *Free Access to the Throne of Grace.* 8. *Communion with the Father and the Son.* 9. *Fellowship with Saints.* 10. *Peace of Conscience.* 11. *Joy in the Holy Ghost.* 12. *A glorious Habitation in this City.* 13. *Divine Protection, or sure Refuge in God.* 14. *A Right to the City Stock, which is the unsearchable Riches of Christ.* Among many other Things respecting the *City Stock,* these Three are comprehended: 1. *A Right to all the Prayers made there.* 2. *To the Promises that belong to it.* 3. *The Stock or Store of Provision laid up in it*; God having said, *He will satisfy h[er] Poor with Bread.* 15. *Liberty, or a proper Right [to] come and drink of, and wash in, and have all oth[er] Blessings of the River before-mentioned.* 16. *A Rig[ht] of Voice in chusing all Sorts of Officers.* 17. *The B[e]nefit of the* City-Guard, *which are an innumerabl[e] Host of Angels.* 18. *An Assurance of Eternal Lif[e.]* 19. *Lastly, When they die, to go to Christ, or have a Dwelling-place with the glorified Saints abo[ve.]*

But let this be observed, That none but Tr[ue]
Citiz[ens]

Citizens are to have these Privileges. If any get in by Policy, whose Hearts are not right with God, let such know they have no Right in these Matters.

Now the Reason why this City holds out, notwithstanding 'tis, and has been long besieged by these mighty Armies, who seem to come up on the Breadth of the Earth against it; is,

1. Because, tho' it be but a small City (comparatively to the City *Sensuality* and Great *Babylon*) yet 'tis a strong City, being (as you have heard) built upon a Rock, and the Throne of God and the Lamb is in it: *God dwelleth in Zion, sing Praises; 'tis the Habitation of his Holiness*: Also, it is a strong Tower, which is the *Name of the Lord*; and this Tower is furnished with glorious Artillery, and other Military Engines of War, to keep off, and destroy the Assailants; for from hence the Almighty distributes *Death, Pestilence*, and *Famine*; by which he makes dreadful Desolation and Havock amongst the proud Enemies, and all graceless Rebels that come against it. The murmuring Cannon never roar'd out more Horror and Amazement to Mortals, than doth the Wrath and Vengeance of an incensed God from hence, upon the *Powers of Darkness*: He has his Hail-stones and amazing Thunder, with Coals of Fire, and dreadful Arrows, which he now and then lets fly with Lightning, to make the Inhabitants of the Earth to tremble. Oh! this is the Place of Security in the Day of Trouble; and Woe to all them that fight against Mount Zion. Doth *Apollyon* think to prevail against this Place? He may indeed tread down the Outward Courts; but the Promise is, *The Gates of Hell shall never prevail against the Church*.

Yet

Yet nevertheless, *Sin*, that bloody Traveller (tho' he lately received a great Blow by *True-Godliness*, and lost his Prey) being forced to retreat in much Disorder, did not desist his Hellish Enterprize against this Town *Religion*, or the *City of God*, but was resolved to try what he could do in a clandestine Way, in order to the spoiling and ruining of the Inhabitants thereof; which to effect, he forthwith makes up to the Walls, and having Information from his Master *Apollyon*, that the Porter, who had the Charge of one of the Gates, was off his Watch, he hasted up to see if he could not get in thereat: The Name of the Porter is, *The Fear of God*; and by this Means he got in Part of those Armies that were headed by *Lucifer*, *Belzebub*, and *Apollyon*, which were made up (as you heard) of the *Lust of the Flesh*, the *Lust of the Eyes*, and the *Pride of Life*; by which Means many within the Town were overcome by *Covetousness*, *Pride*, *Vain Glory*, and *Sensual Pleasures*; and these being overcome by *Surfeiting* and *Drunkenness*, greatly weaken'd the Place, and brought it into Contempt Abroad, opening the Mouths of the Ungodly wide against it; who positively asserted the Inhabitants were as *Worldly Proud* and *Carnal* as those of other Cities.

2. He also prevailed another Way, through Treachery of one Mrs. *Heart*, who like a cursed Incendiary, wrought much Mischief amongst them, and basely corrupted Multitudes of them, by lodging one *Hypocrisy* in their Houses, as notorious a Villain as most in the World.

3. He got also into the City, by the Means of a Beggarly Rascal, called *Sloth*, alias *Security*, a

Idle

The Travels of Ungodliness. 145

...dleness, who took many of them off from their
Duty: These much pleased themselves with the
...are Name of *Religion* and *Christianity*, crying out,
The Temple of the Lord, the Temple of the Lord, &c.
...nd yet were great Strangers to the Life and Power
of *Godliness*, having Lamps, and but little Oil.
...as! how should it be otherwise? For they were
...nsely drawn aside, and deceived by *Sin*, that
...ney neglected their Business, and not with that
Care and Diligence as became them, followed
...eir Trade; and hereby they grew very poor and
...w in Grace, and Spiritual Experiences.

And I think it may not be amiss to shew you
...e how *Sloth*, *Security* and *Idleness*, &c. brought
...Poverty upon them.

...It was by causing them to be much Abroad,
...ling Faults in others, when they should have
...n at Home.

2. By causing them to neglect attending the *Ex-
...ge-Time*; I mean, the solemn Meetings of the
...ens in the *Temple*, where God is worshipped,
...Knowledge may be had how their Affairs go
...aven; and also by putting off (in a lively and
...ful Manner) their Duties, so that they might
...glorious Returns of God's Mercies.

...By not keeping their Books or Accounts care-
...that so they might know whether they got or
...nd hence many of them were ignorant how
...ngs stood between God and their poor Souls.

...ay, and *Peccatum* found out other Ways to
...and spoil the City, by enticing Mrs. *Heart*
...in amongst them one *Unbelief*, alias *Distrust*,
...ersuaded many not to venture much Goods
...p board, Sailing being now grown so dangerous;

144 *The Progress of* SIN: Or,

rous; but to drive a poor, petty, private Trade. Moreover, This home-bred Enemy *Unbelief*, caused some of them to depart from God, and to doubt of his Faithfulness; by which Means their Hands were greatly weakned, and the Enemy prevailed exceedingly.

Also, He surprized some of the Watchmen, filling their Hearts with many sad Thoughts, bringing one upon them, called *Slavish Fear*; who made them too much neglect their Duties, and not maintain their Ground, nor give Warning of the approaching Danger the City was in.

He did much Mischief to the City, by dividing the Inhabitants, or causing of sad Animosities or Divisions amongst them, and thereby alienate their Affections one from another; nay, and some of them were prevailed to Trade with the City *Babylon* for a Parcel of her detestable Traditions; and some others were enticed by the *Lust of the Eyes*, to deal with the City *Sensuality* for some of her abominable Fashions.

Also, Several who were looked upon as her Champions, were secretly and cowardly slain by him; and others were seized and carried away Captive, who sallied out upon the Enemy.

So that in a Word, by one Means or another (by the Help of *Apollyon*) he greatly succeeded his Design upon the *Holy City*.

CH

CHAP. XI.

Shewing how Ungodliness took a Voyage to Sea, and of the Danger he had like to have sustained.

THIS Evil Enemy of Mankind, and restless Traveller, having strangely prevailed both upon the Saint and Sinner, and almost ruined every [Cit]y and Kingdom of the Earth, was at last re[sol]ved to take a Voyage to Sea, and endeavour to [con]quer all those who do Business on the mighty [Dee]p. And no sooner he desired to enter himself on [Ship]board, but all were ready to receive him; the [Ca]ptain, or Master of the Ship embraced him, and [bid] him lie in his Bosom, who learned of him to [tyra]nnize over the poor Seamen, and pinch them [in th]eir Allowance, and abate them of their Wa[ges] by pretending Damage sustained, when indeed [ther]e was none through them; and yet every Sea[man] hugged him also, who taught them to Curse, [Swe]ar, Drink, Whore, and what not; so that he [had] almost obtained a perfect Conquest over them [in] whether Men of War, or Merchants Ships. [But] on a sudden, a mighty Storm arose, and [the] Mariners were sore afraid, fearing this Travel[ler w]as the Cause of it; upon which poor *Consci[ence]* began to cry out, for he lay very heavy in the [mids]t of this great Danger upon him, so that they [resolv]ed to cast him over-board, though *Affection* [woul]d not yield to it, for they loved him dearly. [But th]e Storm increasing, out they cast him; and [now] poor *Conscience* was esteemed the only Com-

G   panion

panion: But it seems, after a little Time, the S
became very calm, which they no sooner percei
but they left off Praying, and took up *Ungodl*
again, and entertained him with as much Jo
ever; insomuch that he now saw he had succe
in every Enterprize, both by Sea and Land, w
so heightned and raised his Spirits, that he br
forth into an amazing, haughty, and Soul-affrig
ing Triumph, to the Effect following.

CHAP. XII.

Sin, or Ungodliness's haughty Triumph

*P*Eccatum, alias *Ungodliness*, by this Time p
ceiving how wonderfully he had prevail
and that there was no Place where-ever he ca
but by one Means or other he got Entertainm
being made the only Joy and Darling of the g
est Part of the whole World, all bowing and b
ing to him, and willingly becoming his Slaves
Vassals, brake forth into a vain-glorious Triu
after this Manner:

*O how I am exalted! Who is like unto me,
be compared with me in the whole Universe!
like a low Shrub, and contemptible Fellow, doth
Godliness look! He is glad to trudge on Foot,
I am mounted on Horseback, whilst Thousands
their Trumpets before me; and behold what renow
Emperors and mighty Potentates do follow
Chains and Fetters, as amazing Trophies of my
conquering Arm! Godliness rejoices when he can
duce here and there two or three Souls; and th*

The Travels of Ungodliness. 147

are but Part of the Refuse of the Earth; but I, mighty I, overcome Millions, nay, subdue Thousands in an Hour, and those of all Sorts: And tho' I use them at my Pleasure, put out their Eyes, and make them grind in my Mill, and do the Devil's Drudgery, yet behold how contented and well pleased the Fools are! they hang upon me, hug me, cleave to me, and by no Means can the Powers Above allure them to leave me. The Thoughts of forsaking me, and losing my sweet Company, is as bad, nay, worse than Death to them: Do you think they have no more Wit, than for the Vanity of a Pardon, or Trifle of inward Peace, or Joys of Heaven, to forget the wonderful Glories, Riches, and Pleasures I offer them on Earth?

But alas! why talk I thus? I do not only make them happy here, as far as the Flesh, World, and Devil can do it, but promise them Bliss also to Eternity, when-ever they die; on easier Terms too, than any Body else will, I am sure. If they will believe me, let them be as wicked as I or Hell can make them, and continue so too until Death seize them; yet with a [Lo]rd have Mercy upon us, they all go to Heaven: [An]d what would they have, trow? I teach them to [li]ve viciously, and yet die happily: And that's the [th]ing I find, they so greatly desire.

And upon this there was a dreadful Noise heard, [an]d terrible Lightning flashed forth in his very Face: [al]so, the Rocks and Mountains seemed to shake [an]d cleave asunder; so that the Monster began to [tre]mble, and cry'd out, Lord Belzebub, What's [the] Matter?

Belzebub. *I can't tell; something more than usual.* With that he suddenly heard one cry like God's [V]engeance, *Seize him, seize him! Lay hold on the*

G 2 *Monster*

148 *The Progress of* SIN: *Or,*
Monster of Pollution, cursed Sin, *and bring him to the Judgment-Seat!*

Upon this, all were silent, and the Devils, who looked as pale as Ashes, whisper'd *Peccatum* in the Ear, to be gone with all Speed; and on a sudden he fled away so swiftly, that before the Officers came to Apprehend him, he hid himself.

CHAP. XIII.

Wherein you have a Hue *and* Cry *after Tyrant* Sin: *Also, who they are that pursue Him: Together with the Manner of his* Apprehention, Arraignment, Tryal, Sentence, *and* Condemnation.

NOW at last, after all the horrid and detestable Villanies committed by the Bloody, Rebellious, and Trayterous Monster *Sin*, we shall proceed, with what Speed we can, towards his *Tryal*: But he, being already alarmed with the News of the Pursuit that was like to be made after him, got away, and hid himself, in some of those Houses where he had been entertain'd. Therefore, the Great and Mighty *Jehovah* (if I may with Reverence speak it) orders a *Hue and Cry*, or rather a *Proclamation* to be issued out to Apprehend him; to the End he may be brought to a Legal Tryal.

Now the *High Constable* that hath received the *Hue and Cry*, is *Divine Providence*.

And for the more easy finding him out, there were Three other Worthies, in the King's Name, warn

The Travels of Ungodliness. 149

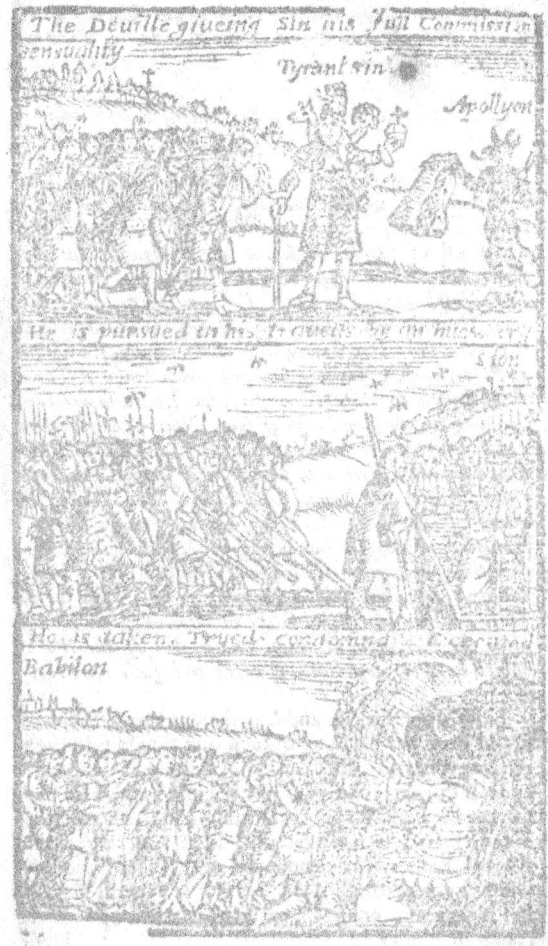

warned to assist him, viz. 1. *Theologue*, Christ's Minister, with his Sword drawn in his Hand. 2. The Operation of the Spirit. And, 3. Enlightned Conscience.

The Proclamation, *or* Hue *and* Cry, *was to this Effect:*

THESE are to Will and Require, and strictly to Command you, in the Great and Dreadful Name of the incensed Majesty of Heaven and Earth, King of Kings and Lord of Lords, to search diligently, find out, and forthwith seize and apprehend that Notorious, Traiterous, and Blasphemous Monster, called Peccatum, alias Sin, alias Ungodliness, alias Iniquity, alias Transgression, &c. who hath been Travelling up and down, from Place to Place, from Country to Country, from Town to Town, from Family to Family, and from one Person to another; breaking all the good Laws of God, Nature, and Nations, and by secret Wiles and Diabolical Devices, and subtil Insinuations, hath deceived, undone, and eternally destroyed many Millions of Souls. As touching his Person, his Name sufficiently describes him: He is a strange Monster, transforming himself into almost what Shapes he pleases: Sometimes appearing like a Lyon, sometimes like a Dove; but most commonly like a Serpent, with a Sting at his Tail, and the Terrestrial Globe in his Hand: which signifies the Pleasures, Honours, and Riches of the World, which he offers as a Bait, to catch or beguile his Prey.

Now, upon the *Hue* and *Cry*, there are large and wonderful Promises made to all such that should fully, readily, and heartily discover him; and, to the uttermost of their Power, endeavour to seize and apprehend him, so that he might be put to Death. And, on the other Hand, there are most dreadful Threats of Wrath and Eternal Punishment denounced on all such who shall willingly or wittingly hide, cover, or conceal him, or not ingenuously confess him, and yield him up into the Hands of Justice.   Upon

Upon which very Account, the *High-Constable, Divine-Providence*, with his Attendants, went forth to search, find out, and apprehend the cursed Traveller, and implacable Enemy of God. But O! the Subtilty he used to blind the Eyes of poor Mortals, so that he might not be discovered! For lo, every suspicious House is now searched, where he had been entertained; some of which I shall here mention, with the strange Devices they used to conceal him; every one almost having got a Cloak to cover him.

The first Place they searched, was *Youth-shire*; and the Cry was, *Is there none here have entertained* Sin, *that horrid Enemy of God?* Immediately *Theologue* knocked at one Door, and at another Door, where young hectoring Gallants lived, and demanded if they had not let him into their Houses, viz. (their Hearts) and made him their Companion, hugging him in their Bosoms, and letting him rule and sway the Scepter over them? No, God forbid, *said one*; Far be it from me *saith another*: Do you think I am such a Villain? What means then (saith *Theologue*) *the Bleating of the Sheep in my Ears?* Are you not Swearers, unclean Persons, Gamesters, Drunkards, &c. They all replied, to excuse and hide him, 'Who, Sir, is without *Sin*? And though you will not Swear, yet, may be, you'll Lye; and as touching those Things of which you speak, they are but Tricks of Youth. Alas! That which you call our Luxury and Lasciviousness, is but our Gayeties and pleasant Pastimes; and that which you call Prodigality, is but a true noble and generous Spirit.'

Now *Conscience* being asleep in these Houses, or otherwise stifled, none of them would confess him; nor will they ('tis to be feared) till *Divine Providence* comes to search for him on his Black, Pale, or Red Horse of Blood, Famine, Pestilence, and Death; and then they must expect no Mercy.

After this, the *Hue* and *Cry* came into the Town of *Riches*, and the Traveller was searched for under the

Name of *Covetousness*; but here was not one that knew him: Nay, so far (I will assure you) they were from giving him quiet and loving Entertainment, that they cry'd out against him with open Mouth, calling him a vile and cursed Enemy; but in the mean Time they hid him under the Cloak of *Thriftiness* and *Good Husbandry*.

The next Place they searched, was the House of Mrs. *Gay Cloaths*, alias *Haughty-Heart*, for the cursed Traveller, under the Name of *Pride*: But she presently deny'd him, or that she had any Love for him; tho' (she said) May be sometimes he may, like a cunning bold Villain, rush into my Company. And further, to hide and conceal him, and make Excuses for him, she said, That her New Fashions were very comely; and God having given her a fair and beautiful Skin, why might she not shew it by her naked Breasts and Shoulders? Is it any where forbidden? Besides, saith she, There are some *Women* and *Virgins* of the *Daughters of Sion*, which follow the Fashions, and go in the same Manner; and if they thought it was Unlawful, they sure would not do it: And truly, Sir, for these *Bulls, Towers, Shades, Curlings* and *Crispings*, with *rich Rings* and *Jewels*, and other *fine Ornaments*, both for *Body, House*, and *Bed*, we think they are very neat, handsome, and pretty Things, and harmless no doubt; For the *Pride* you speak of, lies not in the Mode nor Fashion, but in the Heart: Besides, God (saith she) you cannot deny, doth allow many Things for Ornaments.

Theologue. Madam, I fear, notwithstanding all your plausible Stories, and near Allegations, we shall find the Traveller hid in your House, not only under the Name of *Pride*, but by several Names besides.

For if *Pride, Impudence,* and *Uncleanness* too, are not lurking within, you do very foolishly to hang out the Signs of them. *Tertullian* hath told you plainly, That *Nakedness of the Breast is Adultery*; and tho' it is possible such as go so may be honest, yet but few that see them will believe it.

Wha

The Travels of Ungodliness. 153

What have you, Madam, to say for yourself? Is this the modest Apparel the Apostle willeth Women that profess *Godliness*, to go in? Doth this Mode become Christians? Is it a Sign (speak) of *Shame-facedness*, *Modesty*, and *Sobriety*, which your Garbs and Gestures always should signify, or of the contrary? *Conscience*, I will appeal to thee, Is not *Pride* lodged in this Gentlewoman's House.

Conscience. Sir, He is also.

Theologue. Commit her, and the Tyrant with her, into the *Constable*'s Hands, that they may both appear at the Day of Tryal.

After this they proceeded farther, and the House of one *Fair Speech*, alias *False Tongue*, was searched for him, by the Name of *Lying*; and there he was found hid under the Cloak of *Equivocation*; he not remembring that Word, *Thou shalt speak the Truth unto thy Neighbour in thy Heart*.

The House of *Toss-Pot* they searched for him, by the Name of *Drunkenness*; but there he was found hid under the Cloak of *Good-Fellowship*.

The House of Mrs. *Superstition* they searched for him; but there he was hid under the Cloak of *Good Order* and *Decency*. And the Excuse they had for him was, *'Tis no where forbid*, &c. forgetting *Nadab* and *Abihu*, Lev x. 1, 2.

The House of Mr. *Idolater* was searched, and there he was hid under Abundance of *Images*: The Cloak was, *They helped Devotion*, and 'twas not the *Image* they worshipped, but *God* and *Christ*, in and by the *Image*.

Mount *Sion* was searched, and there he was found in the House of *Formality*, hid under the Cloak of *Religion* and *Seeming Godliness*, by the Name of *Hypocrisy*; and if you would know by what Means he was discovered, read the *Travels of True Godliness*, Chap. IX.

The *Backslider*'s House they searched for him, and there he was found hid under the Cloak of *Human Prudence*, by the Name of *Apostacy*, though the Cause was *Slavish-Fear*, *Self-Love*, and *Unbelief*, &c.

The Houses of *Presumptuous Sinners* were searched, and there *Sin* was found hid under the fair Mantle of *Vain Hope in God's Mercy*.

The House of *Goodman Country* they searched for him, by the Names of *Ignorance*, *Unbelief*, *Hardness of Heart*, *Sloth*, *Idleness*, *Worldly Cares*, &c. But here he was found hid under the Cloak of *Self-Conceit*, with *Good Wishings* and *Wouldings*, *The Lord help us*, *I shall do better when God gives me his Grace*, *My Heart is good*, and, *'tis well if you do no worse? Are you wiser than your Fore-fathers?* &c.

Legalist's House was searched, and there he was found hid under the Cloak of *Self-Righteousness*.

Mr. *Erroneous*'s House of the Town of *Heresy* was searched, and there *Sin* was found hid under the plain Cloak of *Yea* and *Nay*, with *Pretended Zeal*, and *Seeming Sanctity*.

Besides these, every Town, City, Village, and House was searched, where-ever he had been entertained.

But because I shall not have Room, I must say no more as to his Apprehension: But he being in Hold in the *Chief Constable*'s Hand, and other Officers, we shall haste to his Tryal: For hark! the Trumpets sound already, and the Judge is just gone to the Bench.

The Jury Summoned were these following.

New-Man,	Vehement-Desire,
Sound-Judgment,	Fiery-Zeal, of the Town
Divine-Reason,	of Knowledge,
Enlightned-Understanding,	Right Faith,
Godly Fear,	True-Love,
Holy-Revenge,	Impartiality.
Spiritual-Indignation,	

Immediately after the *Jury* was Impannell'd, and the Commission open'd, the Charge given, &c. the Prisoner was called to the Bar, and his Indictment was Read; which run to this Effect:

Sin

Sin, thou Monster of Iniquity, hold up the Hands. Thou art here Indicted by the Name of Peccatum, *alias* Sin, *alias* Transgression, *alias* Iniquity, *alias* Heresy, *alias* Idolatry, *alias* Unbelief, *alias* Adultery, (*and by a Multitude of Names besides*) *That thou being the Child of the Devil, and an Enemy to all Righteousness, hast Traytorously conspired with* Apollyon, *against the God of Heaven, and mortally wounded the whole Lump of Mankind, as soon as ever thou camest into the World; and since that Time, like a most barbarous and bloody Tyrant, hast gone ranging and roaring up and down, committing all the horrid and fearful Crimes and Villainies that the Heart of Man can imagine; so that, in a Word, thou art here Indicted for, and Charged with, all and all sorts of* Treasons, Murders, Massacres, Idolatries, Heresies, Incests, Sodomies, Adulteries, Perjuries, Blasphemies, Wars, Desolations, &c. *to the utter Destruction of the Bodies and Souls of Millions of Millions of Men, Women, and Children, contrary to the Peace, and to the great Dishonour of the Sacred Majesty of the King of Heaven and Earth. What say'st thou, Guilty or not Guilty?*

Clerk. Sir, What dost thou say, Guilty or not Guilty?

Sin. Not Guilty.

Cryer. Call *Adam*, late of *Paradise.*

Here he is, My Lord.

Judge. Come, Old Father, What can you say against *Sin*, the Prisoner at the Bar?

Adam. My Lord, I have this to say:

First, That he made me become a Rebel and Traytor to the King's Majesty, my most Glorious Sovereign, and ever Blessed Creator: For tho' it is true, *Apollyon* did first entice me by his Subtilty, to rebel; yet had it not been for this foul Monster, he could have done me no Hurt. 'Twas *Sin*, My Lord, that overcame me, and caus'd me to break that Law of my Creator, and so to stoop, believe, and be subject to the Devil, rather than God; for by this Means he robb'd me of God's Image (for he is a Thief, as well as a Traytor.) Nay, and not only so, but he robb'd me of Union and Communion with God too, and made my Creator become mine Enemy; yea, it was for his Sake that I was turned out of Paradise: And that which is also very grievous to me to think upon, he by that one Act, murder'd me (in a base and horrible Manner) and all my Posterity, both Soul and Body. I could say much more, and aggravate his Crime under Ten or Twelve Particulars.

Cryer. Call Mrs *Soul* of *Man shire.*

Soul. Here, My Lord.

Judge. What can you say, most noble Lady, against *Sin,* the Prisoner at the Bar?

Soul. My Lord, I was at first the fairest and beautifullest Virgin that ever had a Being on Earth, and was the Praise of God's Creation, in whom his own Image most gloriously shone forth: There was, My Lord, no Stain, Spot, nor ill Feature in my lovely Face; and all my Faculties were pure, holy, and chaste, being free from the least Tincture of Filth, Folly, or Corruption; but this Hellish and Bloody Villain, the Prisoner at the Bar, secretly stole upon me, and in a shameful Manner defiled me; and not only so, but put out my Eyes, and wounded me in a Barbarous Manner in every Part; and he being a rotten and filthy Monster, I was poisoned by him; so that I am now cover'd all over with Corruption and loathsome Stink, insomuch, that if any did but behold me in the State this Enemy hath left me, they would loath to look upon me. Nay, My Lord, he hath given me my Death's Wound too: for as I am a Spirit, he has spiritually slain me, by depriving me of the Life and Light of God's sweet Countenance, which once I enjoyed; so that I lie as one dead in the cursed Arms of this polluted Monster. And moreover, My Lord, I had but one poor Cottage left me to dwell in, and the Prisoner at the Bar turned me out of it, and exposed me to be cast into a Lake of Fire.

Cryer. Mr. *Body* of *Man-shire*--- He appeared.

Judge. What can you say, Mr. *Body,* against *Sin,* the Prisoner at the Bar?

Body.

Body. I was once a very lovely Creature, none exceeded me in God's nether Creation, save that precious Lady (and Companion of mine) who spoke last; I had no Blemish in me, being as sound as a Fish, having Health without Sickness, Strength without Weakness; my Labour also was without Wearisomness. In a Word, I was in a perfect State, and needed nothing to make me happy; being also free from all Things that could annoy or disturb me. But lo, on a sudden this Villain, the Prisoner at the Bar, by his Hellish Subtilty, overcame poor Lady *Soul,* who dwelt with me; and presently next to her, poor I went to the Wall; for he brought in upon me a whole Army of evil Humours, which so corrupted my Blood, &c. that I am invaded, and continually plagued with all manner of sad tormenting and loathsome Diseases; with Blindness, Deafness, Lameness, &c. so that my Life is but Pain and Wearisomness to me. When 'tis Night, I cry, O! when will it be Morning? And when it is Morning, I cry, Would to God it was Evening. My Lord, 'Tis He that hath brought this upon me, and more than this; for he hath let in another Enemy upon me, that grinds me e'er he has done, as small as Dust; nay, makes meer Dung and Filth of me, which Men loath to look upon; for Worms breed on me, and therefore they cover me under Ground: Nay, My Lord, he tears my poor little Babes to Pieces by grievous Diseases, as *Convulsions, Small-Pox,* &c. and sends them from the Breasts to the Grave, without any Pity.

Cryer. Call *Whole Creation.*——Here he is.

Judge. Creation, What can you say against *Sin?*

Creation. My Ground, that was made good, is now by him become barren and unfruitful: Nay, for his Sake, my Great Creator hath curs'd me, so that I bring forth Briars and Thorns, and many other hurtful and venomous Creatures.

Judge. Alas, poor *Creation!* I pity thee with my whole Heart, (O cruel Tyrant!) But it will not be long e'er thou art deliver'd from the *Bondage of Corruption*, into the *glorious Liberty of the Children of God*.

Cryer. Call *Holy Decalogue* of Mount *Sinai*.

Decalogue Here, My Lord.

Judge. What can you say, Renowned *Decalogue*, against *Sin*, the Prisoner at the Bar?

Decal. Most Sacred Judge, I am (as you know) that Holy and Just Law which *Jehovah* gave forth to restrain and curb this cursed Traytor; but he hath in a fearful Manner torn, broke, and wickedly violated me in every Part and Branch of me. And this in short, is what (My Lord) I have to say.

Cryer. Call Mr *Evangelist*.

Mr. *Evangelist*, What can you say against *Sin*?

Evan. My Lord, my Heart sinks in me to see him; but I am glad he is brought to his Tryal.

Judge. Why, what's the Matter; what hath he done?

Evan. Done! He hath by wicked Hands crucified and slain the Lord of Life and Glory.

Upon this, many were in Amaze; *Lord!* says one, *What a Malefactor have we here!*

Cryer. Call in the King's own Daughter, the Blessed Spouse and Wife of the *Lamb*: Come into the Court.

She appeared in her mournful Garments, *yet all Glorious within; and her Cloathing was wrought Gold.*

Judge. What can you say, most Virtuous Lady, against *Sin*, the Prisoner at the Bar?

King's Daughter. My Lord, I have many Things to witness against him.

First. He did what lay in him, to hinder my being Espoused to *Jesus Christ*, my Lord and glorious Husband.

2dly, No sooner, at any Time, that I have brought forth any Child of the *New Covenant*, but he with open Mouth seeks to devour it; and if he cannot do that, then he labours to spoil its Growth, and deface its Beauty.

But, My Lord, 'tis impossible I should now recite the Hundredth Part of what I have to charge him with: But here is a credible Gentleman in the Court, called

Ancient

160 *The Progress of* SIN: Or,

Ancient and *Modern Records*; who can make out much more against him, than what I have said.

Judge. Poor *Zion!* I pity thy sorrowful Condition; but do not be discouraged, his Time is but short

Cryer Mr. *Ancient* and *Modern Records*, of the Country of *Humane*——Here.

Judge. Come, Sir, What is it you can testify against *Sin*, &c.

Ancient Records. Waggoners, Whip on.

Judge. What do you mean? Is this a fit Answer for one of your Years, in such a Place?

Ancient. Most Reverend Judge, I have here at Hand more than a Hundred Waggon Loads of Books, which are of good Credit, that are filled full of the horrid Deeds of this bloody Villain at the Bar, if you will be pleased to have them read.

Judge. That is impossible to be done now, 'tis a Work for many Years; you must repeat some Particulars.

Ancient Records. My Reader can do it, My Lord, whose Name is *Historian*.

Cryer. Historian, come into Court——Here.

Judge. What have you to say against *Sin*, the Prisoner at the Bar? Friend, you must be brief in your Evidence.

Historian. My Lord, I have read much of Mr. *Ancient* and *Modern*'s Testimony; I mean, the Writings of worthy Men, who lived in several Ages of the World, whose Credit and Authority is generally received by all; and there I find such an Account given of the Acts, Deeds, and Cruelties of this Enemy at the Bar, that 'twou'd make a Man tremble to think of: For he hath caused most *horrid Treasons, Plots, Conspiracies, Rebellions, Wars,* &c. *setting one Kingdom against another, Neighbour against Neighbour, the Father against the Son, and the Son against the Father*; yea, he hath filled the whole Earth with all Manner of *Filth and cursed Debauchery, Blood and Violence, Stealing, Cheating, Deceiving, and Destroying both Body and Soul too*; hath been I find,

The Travels of Ungodliness. 161

his Practice; so that he hath not only been a Plague [to] the Church, but also to the whole World. I could [give] you a more particular Account, if your Lord[ship] please to hear it.

Judge. No, Mr. *Historian,* you have said enough.

Cryer. Call *Theologue,* Christ's Minister.

Theol. Here, My Lord.

Judge. Sir, you are summon'd hither to give in your [Te]stimony against *Sin*; pray, therefore, in a concise Manner, open what Evils you know he hath done, or is guilty of, whether *Treasons, Murders, Felonies, &c.*

Theol. My Lord, that I am ready to do.

First, I shall proceed somewhat in a different Manner (as to my Evidence against him) to those worthy Persons who have been already called.

My Lord, He is so vile and evil, that there is no Good in him; he is indeed, the Plague of Plagues; we had far better God should let in upon us all his fearful Judgments, as Famine, Pestilence, and Sword, &c. than to give us up to the Rule, Tyranny, and Dominion of *Sin*.

Judge. I thank you, good Mr. *Theologue,* you have said enough.

Cryer. Call Madam *Grace,* and all her Daughters, *Faith, Hope, Charity, Patience, Prudence, Temperance, Sobriety, Chastity, &c.*

Here, My Lord, we are all.

Judge. Come, virtuous Lady, what can you say for my Sovereign Lord the King, against the Prisoner at the Bar?

Grace. My Lord, I am of a Noble Descent and Parentage, being begotten and born from Above; but [th]is Villain, as much as lay in him, endeavoured to [hin]der both my Conception and Nativity.

Cryer. Call Mrs. *Grace's* Eldest Daughter, *Saving-*[Faith].

Faith. Here, My Lord.

Judge. Most precious *Faith.* What have you to say?

Faith. This Villain, hath by many cunning De[vice]s made me contemptible, as if I were of no higher Pedigree,

162 *The* Progress *of* SIN: *Or,*

Pedigree, than of a Human Extraction, or begotten refined Nature.

2. He has made me so feeble and weak (by hindering me of that good Nourishment God hath provided for me) that I can scarce go alone; he lies so heavy upon me, that I can hardly look up. Moreover, he is in upon me oftentimes, one *Despond*; who, like a merciless Tyrant, knocks me down at one Blow.

Pray call my Sister *Hope*.

Judge. Fair Damsel, What can you testify against this Prisoner?

Hope. My Lord, He hath often forced me almost to let go my Anchor-hold, by which Means the poor Ship, *Soul*, hath been upon the rough Waves of a tempestuous Sea, and in Danger every Hour of being broken in Pieces, and utterly lost upon the pernicious Rocks of either *Presumption* or *Despair*. Besides, My Lord, He hath very near in Time of great Tribulation, destroyed my Two Sisters, *Patience* and *Experience*.

Judge. Is this so, Mrs. *Patience*?

Patience. Yes, my Lord; for in Times of Tribulation, this Enemy hath let in one *Discontent*, and his Brother *Repine*; by which Means I was turned out of Doors, and lost the Help of *Experience*, who is a dear Friend to my Sister *Hope*.

Judge. Were ever virtuous Damsels thus basely used?

Mrs. *Charity*, What have you to say against the Prisoner at the Bar?

Charity. Most serene Judge, This cursed Tyrant hath so prevailed, that I am become as one almost dead; whosoever feels me, shall find me even Clay-cold. I am, my Lord, through his Means, also grown much out of Esteem; most being weary of my Company. Besides, I and all my Sisters stand in Fear of our Lives for as he goes by the Name of *Covetousness*, he hath tempted to murder us all together: Nay, and he hath put out of Joint both the Arms of my Sister *Bounty*, and hath almost broken my Back, and the Back of my Sister
Liberali-

The Travels of Ungodliness. 163

lity, and hath forced poor *Hospitality* out of Doors; [se]t all People so against her, that none hardly will [receive] her, or take her in. But I'll say no more, but [give] way to my Sisters, *Sobriety* and *Temperance*.

[Jud]ge. Well, what can you say, beautiful Virgins, [against] *Sin*, the Prisoner at the Bar?

[Sob]riety. My Lord, I and my Sister were employed [to ke]ep the House of every Christian Man, and to mo[derat]e his Mind in all his Affairs: But lo, on a sudden, [an u]nruly Fellow, and Enemy of God and all Good[ness,] let in upon us a vile Wretch, called *Inordinate* [Desi]res; who had no sooner got in his Foot, but poor [we] went to the Wall, and were laid weltering in our [Blo]od; for he led him out to use the Creatures to Ex[cess] in Eating, Drinking, Sleeping, Recreation, Pleasures, &c. which our Natures could never endure.

Judge. Come forth (*Chastity*) Sweet heart; Have [yo]u any Thing to charge the Prisoner with?

Chastity. Alas! My Lord, my Heart is ready to [b]reak to see him; for like a wicked Beast as he is, he [w]ould have committed a Rape upon me: Lord help [m]e, my Spirits are almost gone.

Judge. Give her a Cordial. Come, Damsel, What [is] that you say?

Chastity. My Beauty is (as you see) like the Sun, and [a]m fairer than the driven Snow; and I have also a [pure] and spotless Mind; but this Monster, having [kick]ed down my two poor Sisters, *Sobriety* and *Temp[eranc]e*, by the Excess of Gluttony, Drunkenness, &c. [the]y was let in two of his own base Offspring, *viz.* [Who]ring and *Wantonness*, and they had almost forced [me. H]owever, I lay in a great deal of Danger, and [hardly] escaped with my Life.

[Jud]ge. Have you any other Sister that hath not been [here?]

[Chas]tity. Yea, my Lord, here is my Sister *Prudence*.
[Jud]ge. Come, Mrs. *Prudence*, Pray declare what [you h]ave to say against the Prisoner.

Prudence.

Prudence. My Lord, he has done me as much [wrong?]
as any of my dear Sisters. 'Tis I who teach Me[n]
W[o]men to make good use of their Seasons and O[ppor]-
t[u]nities, for the Good of their Souls and Bodies [but]
this cruel Tyrant hath often endeavoured to destr[oy me]
by letting in two other Enemies, and base bred V[illains,]
Idleness and *Vain-Hope*; so that the *Ant*, by a c[ertain]
Instinct of Nature, learns more Wisdom in prov[iding]
her Fruit in the Summer, and gathering her Meat in [Har-]
vest, than I can reach Mankind. Nay, my Lord, [I]
can hardly (now-a-days) find a Service, (tho' none
the worst Housewives) in City or Country; for if P[eo]-
ple would entertain me, I would soon *cloath them*
with Silk and Purple, and make them Coverings of Tapestr[y.]

Judge. I know, *Prudence*, thou art a painful Maide[n,]
Many Women have done virtuously, but thou and t[hy]
Sisters have excelled them all. I accept of thy Evidence, and will see Justice done thee and them too,
with a Vengeance.

Cryer. Call Mr. *Conscience.*
Conscience. Here, My Lord.
Judge. Come, *Conscience*, What can you say for ou[r]
Sovereign Lord the King, against *Sin*, the Prisoner a[t]
the Bar?

Conscience. There hath, My Lord, been a great de[al]
said and witnessed against him already; but I can (nevertheless) charge him with such kind of horrid Cri[mes]
that none knows of besides me, and the M[aje]st[y of]
Heaven. He is truly, a Monster of Wickedn[ess,]
committing all Deeds of Darkness; for tho' he is [evi]-
dent enough, yet there are some of his Treasons, M[ur]-
ders, Incests, Adulteries, and horrid Combinati[ons]
that *Apollyon* himself is ashamed of, or rather afraid s[hould]
come to Light. He hath erected, my Lord, his T[hrone]
in the House of one M[r]. *Heart*, and there he som[e how]
hatches, and contrives all manner of heinous Cr[imes]
and unknown filthy Abominations; as Murders, [Adul]-
teries, Fornications, False-Witnesses, Blasphemies,

The Travels of Ungodliness. 165

Heresies, Lasciviousness, Envy, Malice, Re-
and what not. Much more I could say, My
but that I am not willing to tire the Court.

?. You have performed your Part in few Words.
Here are many more Witnesses, My Lord
I cannot bear him now; there hath been
said against him already. Come, vile Traytor,
unster of Wickedness. What hast thou to say for
why Sentence of Death shou'd not pass upon

My Lord, I have much to say, [illegible] I
be abused and be-ly'd after this [illegible]
Be-ly'd, Villain? Wherein [illegible]
My Lord, All manner of Evils [illegible]
ted under the Sun, is charged [illegible]
es against Me, whereas the Evidence [illegible]
een the chief Instrument that hath [illegible]

p. But how? How came he to be a [illegible] He
good Angel at first, and therefore [illegible]
what Means he is made so vile as to [illegible]
ernise Deeds against the God of Heaven? Did
at first deceive him? I must tell you, hath
ade very evident against and against that You
m a Devil, so that the Evils and Mischief he
ae is just to be charged upon you

Aye, but yet if it please you, I am wronged;
n of the Wickedness that has been, and whence
has been occasioned by Man's own evil Heart.
e. 'Tis a vain Thing to use this Reference for
re. Pray how came the Heart of Man to be so?
Was it not a good and honest Heart? [illegible]
into it [illegible]
you any Thing more to say? [illegible]

have got a Pardon here for many [illegible]
from *His Holiness.* P. O. [illegible]
of a Council to plead for [illegible]

Prudence. My Lord, he has done me as much W[rong]
as any of my dear Sisters. 'Tis I who teach Me[n and]
Wo[men] to make good use of their Seasons and O[ppor]
t[u]nities, for the Good of their Souls and Bodies[; but]
this cruel Tyrant hath often endeavoured to destr[oy me]
by letting in two other Enemies, and base bred Vil[lains,]
Idleness and *Vain-Hope*; so that the *Ant*, by a c[ertain]
Instinct of Nature, learns more Wisdom in prov[iding]
her Fruit in the Summer, and gathering her Meat in [Har]
vest, than I can teach Mankind. Nay, my Lord, [I]
can hardly (now-a-days) find a Service, (tho' none [of]
the worst Housewives) in City or Country; for if P[eo]
ple would entertain me, I would soon *cloath them*
with Silk and Purple, and make them Coverings of Tapestr[y.]

Judge. I know, *Prudence*, thou art a painful Maide[n,]
Many Women have done virtuously, but thou and t[hy]
Sisters have excelled them all. I accept of thy Evi[-]
dence, and will see Justice done thee and them too[,]
with a Vengeance.

Cryer. Call Mr. *Conscience.*

Conscience. Here, My Lord.

Judge. Come, *Conscience,* What can you say for ou[r]
Sovereign Lord the King, against *Sin,* the Prisoner a[t]
the Bar?

Conscience. There hath, My Lord, been a great dea[l]
said and witnessed against him already; but I can (ne[-]
vertheless) charge him with such kind of horrid Cri[mes]
that none knows of besides me, and the Maj[esty of]
Heaven. He is truly a Monster of Wickedne[ss,]
committing all Deeds of Darkness; for tho' he is ev[i]
dent enough, yet there are some of his Treasons, [Mur]
ders, Incests, Adulteries, and horrid Combinati[ons]
that *Apollyon* himself i[s] ashamed of, or rather afraid s[hould]
come to Light. He hath erected, my Lord, his Th[rone]
in the House of one M[rs.] *Heart,* and there he for[ges,]
hatches, and contrives all manner of heinous Cr[imes]
and unknown filthy Abominations; as Murders, [Adul]
teries, Fornications, False-Witnesses, Blasphemies

The Travels of Ungodliness. 165

Heresie, Lasciviousness, Envy, Malice, Re-
and what not. Much more I could say, My
but that I am not willing to tire the Court.
v. You have performed your Part in few Words.
Here are many more Witnesses. My Lord
I cannot bear them now; there hath been
said against him already. Come, vile Traytor,
master of Wickedness. What ha't thou to say for
why Sentence of Death shou'd not pa's upon

My Lord, I have much to say........ all I
be abused and be-ly'd after this......
Be-ly'd, Villain! Wherein?......
My Lord, All manner of Evil......was
ed under the Sun, is charged (as it were) fa-
es against Me; whereas the Devil......
een the chief Instrument that hath done great
it.......................

But hark! How came he to be a....? He
good Angel at first, and therefore let us under-
what Means he is made so vile as to act so of
rrible Deeds against the God of Heaven?......
at first deceive him? I must tell you, Goliath
ade very evident again and again, that You
m a Devil, so that the Evil and Mischief he
ne is just to be charged upon you......
Aye, but even if it please you, I am wronged;
of the Wickedness that has been, hath it not
has been occasioned by Man's own evil Heart.
a. 'Tis a vain Thing to use this Reply......
re. Pray, how came the Heart of Man, (who
Was in once good and honest Heart) to run
into it......
you any Thing more to say?......

have got a Pardon here for many Crimes This
has from *His Honour,* B. O......
of a Council to plead for......

Judge. Who would you trust your Cause with

Sin. Ignatius Loyola, Bellarmine, &c.

Judge. This Court can't admit of Criminals Council for a Malefactor, who have been cashiered degraded long ago.

Yet we will give you all the fair Play imagin Come, we will weigh the Validity or Strength of Pardon. Pray, how came *His Holiness* to have Power to pardon you; since 'tis positively said, *can forgive Sins but God?* Tho' 'tis granted a Man forgive his Brother that has trespassed against him far as he is injured thereby; yet he can't forgive Offence, as 'tis against God: But you are charged the highest Treasons that ever were committed the Majesty of Heaven; and tho' a Sinner may b given, yet *Sin* must die; that was ever the Sense of just Law and Law-maker, by which you are Trye

Sin Good my Lord, pity me, a Psalm of Me Do not cast away an Old Man; 'tis near Six Thou Years ago since I was born.

Judge. 'Tis high Time therefore to rid the So Man of you. I must proceed to your Sentence.

Upon this the Attorney-General, *Divino-J* stood up, and spoke to this Purpose: *My Lord, quire Judgment not only to pass against the Prison but also against the Sinner too; for they are guilty Crimes before God, and it stands not consistent Glory and Holiness, that they should be acquitted: fore I in His Name will and command, that the Se of Eternal Death do forthwith pass upon them, and of them; for the Wages of Sin is no less Punishmen they have all broke that just Law that lays them God's Curse, and the Damnation of Hell; neither acquit one Soul of them.*

The Jury presently found him Guilty, and th ner too.

Upon this, O the lamentable Cry that was a those Mortals, whose Consciences were awake

Travels of Ungodliness.

...trembling at the Bar, wringing their Hands, ...like a River gushed from their Eyes, beg- ...their Knees for Pardon and Forgiveness in en- ... the Traveller.

...the King's Sollicitor, *Divine-Mercy*, stood up ...Sinners, but spoke not a Word in Behalf of ...grand Criminal; and spoke to this Purpose: ...*ereon Lord*, I am ordered by his Most Sacred ...nal Majesty, to plead for these self-condemned ...tors; for though *Divine Justice* can shew no ...yet is God Gracious as well as Just; and hath ...Forgiveness to all such Souls who repent un- ...and forsake this cursed Tyrant; therefore ... ...fer such Souls to perish.

...Well, to reconcile you both, and greaten ...my equally, Divine Wisdom in God hath ...a happy and blessed Medium, that so he may ...just as Justice can require, and yet as graci... ...Sinner can desire; This it is: The Lord Je... ...hath in the Sinner's Stead laid down a suffi... ...to make a Compensation for all the Wrongs ...tors have done to the Law, to Justice, ...iness. Therefore the Sentence is this; ...hast been Arraigned, Tryed, and found ...all those bloody, amazing, and abominable ...s Treason, Murder, &c. charged against ...erefore, every Soul, who is thoroughly con- ...its heinous Evil, and doth in Loving, and ...d Entertaining, heartily confess and forsake ...and apply the Virtue of Christ's Blood as the ...edy, he shall live, and be forgiven: But ...die without Mercy, and they, by the Holy ...Spirit, shall crucify her; neither shall they ...Lives and Pardon upon any other Terms; ...they must die, or thou must be slain, mor... ...crucified in them, and by them.

...you who do not this, (pray hear your Sen- ...confess, leave, loath, and utterly forsake

168   *The Progress of* SIN: *Or,*

Sin, that detestable and odious Enemy, and apply the
Virtue of Christ's Blood, as the only Means whereby he
hath satisfied the Justice, and made an Atonement for
you; but shall still love, live in, and cherish that
cursed Monster, shall every one of you remain in the
Hands of Divine Wrath until you die, and then your
Souls shall go to Torment; and in the dreadful Day
of Judgment, Bodies and Souls too, with Sin, which
you have so dearly loved, shall be cast into the Lake
that burneth with Fire and Brimstone, there to remain
with inconceivable Torments for ever and ever.

Upon this, with such Joy that no Tongue is able to
express, some poor Souls took hold of God's gracious
Mercy, and were pardoned. But the greatest Part
made light of all that was said, and seemed to set the
Court at nought, being harden'd in their Sins: So that
the Sentence against their evil Deeds was accordingly
executed; so that they fell into the Hands of Divine
Wrath and Vengeance, and are like to perish for ever
and ever: And thus the TRIAL ended.

FINIS.

N.B. *There is Published A BOOK, Entituled,* Travels *of* true Godliness. *By the*
AUTHOR. *Printed for* W. *johnston, at the Golden-Ball, in Ludgate-Street.*

www.ingramcontent.com/pod-product-compliance
Lightning Source LLC
LaVergne TN
LVHW061215060426
835507LV00016B/1938